T0205024

A GUIDE TO GRIEF

COLE IMPERI
ILLUSTRATED BY
BIANCA JAGOE

KIDS CAN PRESS

To Ruby

Published in Canada and the U.S. by Kids Can Press Ltd.
25 Dockside Drive, Toronto, ON M5A 0B5

Kids Can Press is a Corus Entertainment Inc. company

www.kidscanpress.com

FSC
www.fsc.org
MIX
Paper | Supporting
responsible forestry
FSC® C016245

The artwork in this book was rendered digitally.
The text is set in Minion Pro.

Edited by Patricia Ocampo
Designed by Barb Kelly

Printed and bound in Canada in 7/2024 by Friesens

CM 24 0 9 8 7 6 5 4 3 2 1

Library and Archives Canada Cataloguing in Publication

Title: A guide to grief / written by Cole Imperi; illustrated by Bianca Jagoe.
Names: Imperi, Cole, author. | Jagoe, Bianca, illustrator.
Description: Includes bibliographical references and index.
Identifiers: Canadiana (print) 20230568319 | Canadiana (ebook) 20230568327 |
ISBN 9781525309656 (hardcover) | ISBN 9781525311628 (EPUB)
Subjects: LCSH: Grief — Juvenile literature. | LCSH: Grief in children — Juvenile literature. | LCSH: Bereavement — Juvenile literature. | LCSH: Bereavement in children — Juvenile literature. | LCSH: Death — Juvenile literature. | LCSH: Children and death — Juvenile literature. | LCGFT: Informational works.
Classification: LCC BF723.G75 I47 2024 | DDC j155.9/37083 — dc23

Kids Can Press gratefully acknowledges that the land on which our office is located is the traditional territory of many nations, including the Mississaugas of the Credit, the Anishnabeg, the Chippewa, the Haudenosaunee and the Wendat peoples, and is now home to many diverse First Nations, Inuit and Métis peoples.

"Those who learned to know death, rather than to fear and fight it, become our teachers about life"

- DR ELISABETH KÜBLER-ROSS
On Children and Death, 1983

INTRODUCTION

If you are reading this book, it's probably because you are grieving or know someone who is. And if you have experienced a big loss — someone died or something in your life has changed forever — then you might have heard someone say:

The truth is, you can't "get over" grief. You move forward with grief. It becomes part of you.

This book is a guide through this difficult — sometimes wonderful — process. Just as climbers rely on Sherpas to help them on the difficult trek to the top of Mount Everest, we all need help traveling through our grief.

As a thanatologist (someone who knows about death, dying, grief and loss), I research and teach about these challenging life experiences. And as a chaplain (someone who provides spiritual care), I help people navigate through loss. I have also experienced loss in my own life — people in my family and friend groups have died, and I've also grieved losses in life that aren't connected to a person or animal.

After witnessing others experience grief — and after moving forward with grief myself — I know two things to be true:

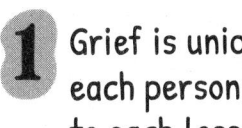 Grief is unique to each person and to each loss.

 Learning about grief makes it less unfamiliar.

I hope to help you navigate your own grief with the compassion and care you need, and I hope to give you some useful information that will make the whole experience less unfamiliar.

As you read this book, if anything is too hard or too difficult, you should take a break and talk to someone you trust. Reading about this stuff might bring up sad memories or confusing questions, and it's important to find someone to help you talk this out. Throughout the book I share contact information and websites to help you connect to people who can help. They're also gathered in the Resources section (p. 179) at the back of this book.

There is a community of people who want you to know you're not alone in these complicated and difficult feelings. My hope is that this book will be one part of your entire community of care.

HOW TO USE THIS GUIDE

Start with Chapter One to understand what grief is.

Move on to Chapter Two if you've experienced a deathloss (the death of a person or animal you love) or to Chapter Three if you've had a shadowloss (a loss *in* life, not *of* life).

If you've experienced both kinds of loss, you will probably want to understand them both. Much like your grief journey, your path through this book might not be simple and straightforward.

You can choose your own path! (But I do recommend everyone start with Chapter One.)

Chapter One 15

This chapter defines grief. Of course, you will define grief for yourself, in your own unique way, because no one has experienced things in exactly the same way that you have. Knowing some basics about grief can help you on your journey and also help you understand what might be happening to others.

Chapter Two 39
Chapter Three 65

These chapters go over two kinds of loss: deathloss and shadowloss. Which one have you experienced?

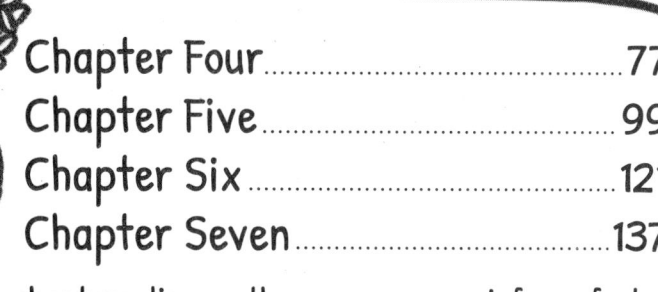

Chapter Four..77
Chapter Five...99
Chapter Six 121
Chapter Seven.......................................137

These chapters discuss the many ways grief can feel (spoiler alert: it's not just sad!), what complicates it and what can help.

Chapter Eight 147
Chapter Nine 159

In these chapters you learn how (and how not) to help others through their grief.

Grief Journal.............172

You might need space to write down what's on your mind. If you feel like writing but don't know what to say, there are prompts to guide you!

A Note for Caregivers.......176

As Grief Guides (for any adults reading this!) walking alongside a grieving young person, you'll want some extra information about your role. There's a special note for you at the back of this book!

LOOK OUT FOR THESE SIGNS ON YOUR JOURNEY

As you move through this book, you'll notice some repeating sections. These are supportive and restful places to take a break. Each section is explained below so you know what to look for.

Carry this with you

Each chapter ends with a summary of the main takeaways and key points.

EXTRA HELP

LOOK FOR THESE WEBSITES, PHONE NUMBERS AND OTHER WAYS TO GET HELP.

MORE RESOURCES ARE ON PAGE 179.

Grief Glossary

Sometimes it feels like grief has its own language. Words or phrases that might be new for you are in bold. You can learn their full definitions on page 174.

These are short exercises and things to do that might be a little bit fun and a lot helpful.

⌒ Loving Kindness ⌒

Sometimes we just need to hear a kind voice. You can say these calming and grounding reminders to yourself whenever you need a little extra support.

THE GRIEF GROUP

Meet five people who are all grieving losses.
You will hear from them throughout this book
as they share their grief stories.

My name is **Alejandro,** and my pronouns are he/him. I really miss my dog, Rubí.

I'm **Bao,** and my pronouns are she/her. My parents divorced. AND I had to move to a new school across town. UGH.

I'm *Emma*. My pronouns are she/her and they/them. The worst thing happened: my mom died. It's been awful without her.

Hey, I'm **JACOB**, and my pronouns are they/them. Life is kinda chaotic with a single mom and our money troubles. But we have lots of friends!

I'm *Diya*. My pronouns are she/her. I lost a friend from school, and my grandfather died.

MOVING THROUGH THE WILDERNESS OF GRiEF

Grief and loss are often things people try to "get through" or ignore, avoiding the uncomfortable parts. It's not that people don't care; it's because they *do* care. They're scared to say the wrong thing and "make things worse." In general, people are uncomfortable talking about death and loss and grief (for all kinds of reasons), so it can feel really lonely if you're dealing with it. People might avoid you, and you might even try to avoid yourself.

This book will tell you what you need to know about grief and loss so you can best support yourself and others. It will show you how grief and loss are normal, natural and challenging parts of being human.

You are part of a new generation of grievers. Let's start talking about endings. It's time to move forward with grief.

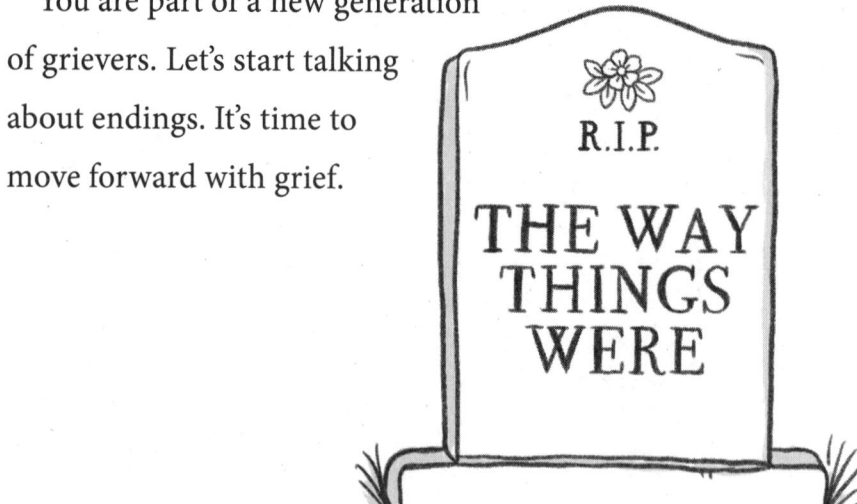

R.I.P.

THE WAY THINGS WERE

EXTRA HELP

CALL OR TEXT 988
IF YOU NEED SOMEONE
TO TALK TO AND ARE IN
THE UNITED STATES
OR CANADA.
THERE IS SOMEONE
THERE FOR YOU 24/7.

Chapter One

GRiEF iN BRIEF

Every single person will experience grief at some point. It is inescapable. Just as we don't get to skip being born, we don't get to skip experiencing grief. It is a part of life, and it is something that changes your life.

Yet for something so common — so universal — it isn't often freely talked about by adults. Have you ever asked an adult about death and they suddenly started acting strangely, whispering "we'll talk about it later" — only later never comes? Many adults are afraid to talk about death with kids. Often, it's not because they are scared of death (death is a normal part of life for all living things — from flowers to people to pets to trees) but because they are scared of scaring you.

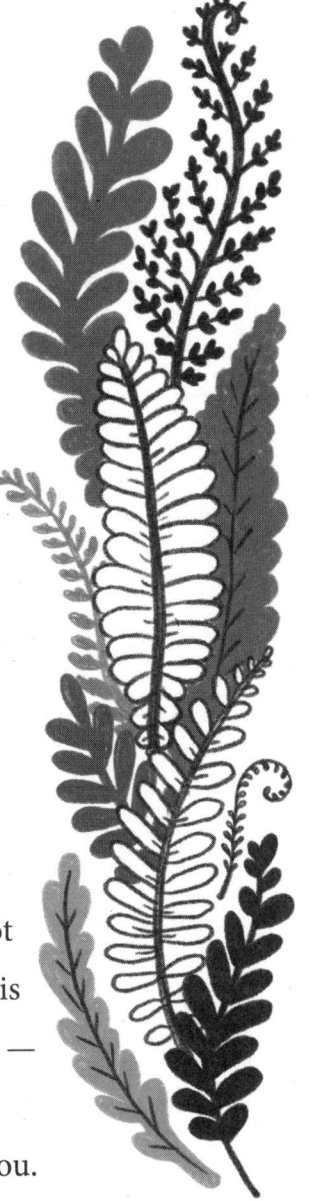

Many adults are afraid of making a young person cry when talking about death, or they're afraid of making a young person feel scared about the world.

Many adults are uncomfortable with sharing their own feelings of sadness and fear with kids because they worry kids won't feel safe if an adult is feeling sensitive or upset. They worry about explaining it in the wrong way or saying it in a way that might not be totally accurate. Death isn't always an acceptable topic of conversation in our society, and so kids who didn't learn how to talk about it grow up to be adults who don't know how to talk about it.

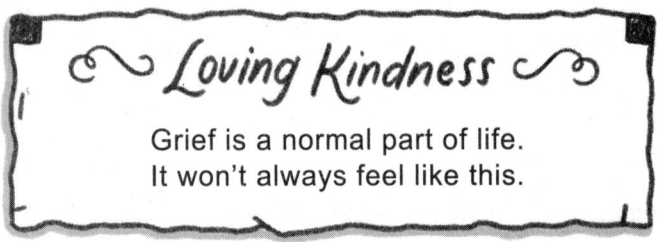

Loving Kindness
Grief is a normal part of life.
It won't always feel like this.

Most young people have questions about death and grief when there has recently been a death or when someone is actively grieving. For the adults in their lives, it can be hard to answer questions or share thoughtful explanations about death and grief when they themselves might also be grieving.

Imagine getting stung by a bee for the first time, right on your little finger. You start crying. It really hurts. The adults around you are trying to calm you down, take the stinger out and keep calm themselves.

Then, in the middle of the noise and pain and confusion, your little brother comes up and asks, "Why do bees sting people? Why does it hurt to get a bee sting? Can bees sting people more than once? Where do bees live?"

It's like that. The best time to answer questions about a bee sting is probably not while someone is actively crying about being stung by one!

It's the same with grief. It can be hard for adults to answer questions about death and dying and grief and loss when they are actively experiencing it.

That's where this book comes in. This book will never be too tired or too upset or too distracted to answer your questions. And while it might not have an answer for every single question you have about death and grief and loss, hopefully it will teach you how to think about those things on your own and help you find answers that work for you. It can probably even help the adults in your life, too.

SO WHAT IS GRIEF?

This might surprise you, but ⨍ **grief** ⨎ is not a feeling.

You can feel sad. You can feel happy. You can feel hopeless. You can feel joyful. Those are all ⨍ **feelings** ⨎. Depending on who you ask and where in the world they are, there are dozens — even hundreds — of different feelings, and each and every one of them can be part of your grief experience.

But grief itself is not a feeling.

You see, grief is actually a process. It's a journey you take. You might go left when someone else goes right. You might need to walk slowly through an overgrown jungle, while another grieving person — even someone grieving the same thing as you — might need to race through an open field. There is literally no one on Earth who has ever skipped over grief. Jesus experienced loved ones dying. Muhammed did, too. So did Michael Jordan, Lionel Messi, Priyanka Chopra, Albert Einstein, Cleopatra and The Rock. This is part of being human. Everyone will grieve at some point in life. And most likely, everyone will grieve more than once.

It's important to understand that grief is the way you uniquely respond to a loss, whether that's a ⨍ **deathloss** ⨎ (Chapter Two) or a ⨍ **shadowloss** ⨎ (Chapter Three). It is a process that includes feelings, but it is not just a feeling.

It would be a lot simpler if grief were just a feeling.

For example, if you feel sad one afternoon, chances are you won't be sad the next morning. Feelings come and go more quickly.

But if you are grieving one afternoon, you will probably be grieving the next day, and the following day and the day after that, and on each of those days, you will have a wide variety of different feelings that keep on appearing and disappearing.

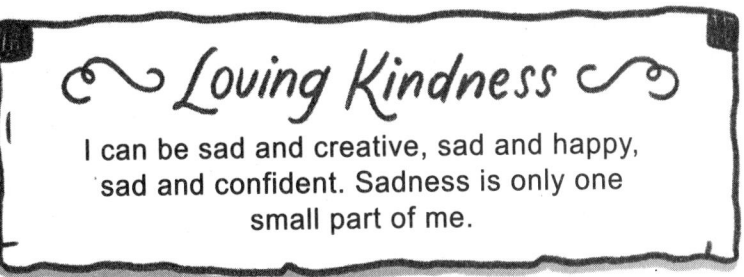

Loving Kindness

I can be sad and creative, sad and happy, sad and confident. Sadness is only one small part of me.

Even though grief is more complicated than any one feeling, it is also just as normal. Both grief and feelings are normal parts of being human. As you continue reading, you'll see how grief is the overall process you experience over time, while feelings make up smaller parts of that grief experience.

WHAT DOES GRIEF FEEL LIKE?

If grief isn't a feeling but is instead a process, how do you know you are grieving? Our bodies and brains send signals that let us know when things have changed within us. These signals are sometimes called **symptoms**, but they can also be described as **signs**.

For example, coughing could be a sign of a cold or just a result of food going down the wrong pipe. Tears could be a sign of sadness or of an allergy attack — or even joy! These signs give us clues we can use to figure out what is going on inside us. When people say "listen to your body," what they really mean is "pay attention to all the signs." When you pay attention to them, you're better able to make healthy choices about how to take care of yourself.

The signs associated with grief can be grouped into six categories. When a person grieves, they may experience signs from all or just some of the categories.

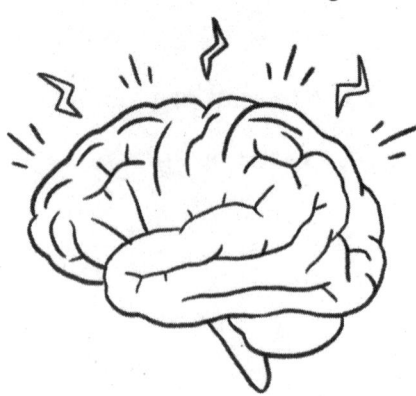

The categories are:

COGNiTiVE SiGNS

The word (cognitive) means "stuff your brain does." It refers to things like memory, attention span, language and how you move your body.

When people are grieving, they might experience some cognitive changes. In other words, the way our brain works might change a little. While these changes might really worry you, know that they are totally normal and only temporary.

Why does your brain do this? Well, to put it simply, when we are grieving, our brains are putting more energy toward understanding the loss. That takes a lot of energy! That energy has to come from somewhere, so the brain has to pull it away from other tasks.

You might notice that you've been having a hard time remembering stuff — even basic things! Maybe you are pretty good at remembering birthdays or putting your homework in your backpack, but while you are grieving you blank out more or miss due dates.

Another sign of grief is a lack of focus. Grieving people may struggle to work on one task for a long time. Getting easily distracted is a normal part of grief.

Someone grieving might say the wrong words. For example, you are in the kitchen and you start to ask, "Where are the apples?" But instead of saying "apples" you say "keys." No matter how hard you try in the moment, you just can't think of the word you want to say. Grief can make your head feel like it's been put in a blender without a lid, leaving you all mixed up with the wrong words spilling out.

Your brain controls how you move your body, right? Going down a staircase. Using your thumbs to play a video game. Picking up your water bottle. Well, while you are grieving you might all of a sudden start feeling clumsier — missing a step, pressing the button for "jump" instead of "crawl," or knocking over your water bottle when you reach to pick it up. This can feel alarming, but again, it is a very normal part of grieving.

These things can happen in any time of stress — not just in grief. It's important to know that grief and stress go hand in hand. It's stressful when someone we love dies or any major change in life happens. Your body will show different kinds of signs when you are under stress, and those signs will give you clues to the kind of care and support that will make you feel better.

PHYSICAL SIGNS

Physical signs that might show up as part of a grief response include feeling really tired (fatigue) or achy all over, or having an uncomfortable tightness in your abdomen (it's called bloating when your body holds extra fluid or gas). You also might have an upset stomach, diarrhea or nausea. Chapped lips are also a physical sign of grief.

There are lots of ways you can take care of those physical signs, and it's a good idea to try a few to see what works best for you.

Try stretching or a gentle walk. Eating lots of snacks or sweets might feel good in the short term but could actually make those signs much worse a few hours later. You'll need to pay attention to see how the signs affect you.

SPiRiTUAL SIGNS

When we experience grief, we might find ourselves considering some big questions: "Is there a God?" or "Why do we exist? What's the point?" Similarly, when grieving, people often struggle with spirituality or the idea of a higher power, a God or a "spirit." They might ask things like "If God loves me, then why did he let my loved one die?"

Grief is like a giant magnifying glass. It makes you notice and think about things you never noticed or thought about before. Things you thought to be true — a certain person would always be there, your life would unfold in a particular way, or if you did X, Y and Z then everything would be fine — are now not, and so you question what else might not be true.

These can be hard questions. It's important to know that most people have asked these same big questions. But you might be scared to ask a friend what they think. You might worry that they will laugh it off or share an opinion that makes you feel worse. This can be a lonely feeling. That's why it can help to ask your parent or guardian, religious leader, school counselor or other trusted adult. Since adults have had more time to experience grief, they might have a way of looking at these questions in a different way than you or in a way that brings you comfort. Even when adults don't have the answers you are looking for, just talking it out can help.

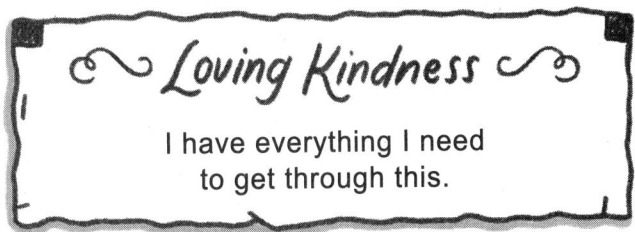

Loving Kindness

I have everything I need
to get through this.

Another way to find spiritual guidance is through books. Most religions have important spiritual books, and these books talk about difficult moments, death and feeling lost. If you are Christian, that book might be the Bible.

If you are Jewish, the Torah. Muslims have the Quran. Hindus have the Upanishads and the Vedas. There are many more books belonging to other traditions.

Books of poetry and fiction can bring comfort as well. Artistic words painted across a page can sometimes make a whole lot more sense than just about anything else. Reading about characters living through enormous challenges can bring comfort and a source of inspiration for your own journey.

Music and song lyrics might be something you connect with. There's a reason that songs are played at important life events — from weddings to graduations to funerals. You might have certain songs that remind you of certain people or even specific times in your life. They can be meaningful, moving and help us connect with our big feelings as well as with our communities. Music can help us keep our grief moving.

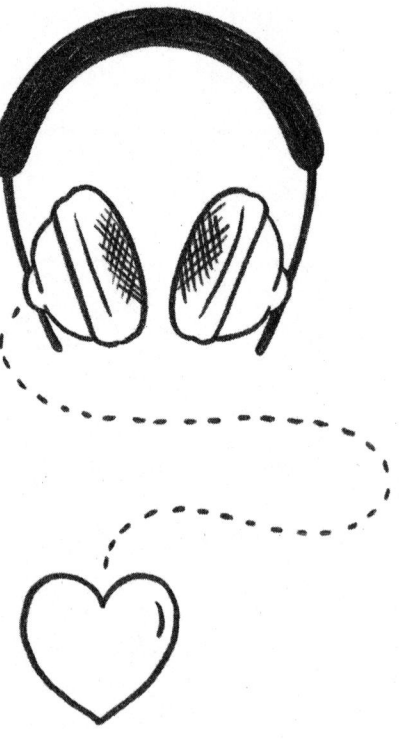

BEHAVIORAL SiGNS

Behavioral signs have to do with how you act — your behaviors. All kinds of behaviors can be affected in all sorts of ways, but we'll talk about only a few in this section.

Sleep is one of the most common things to be disrupted when grieving. It's normal to have a poor night (or many poor nights) of sleep — you might struggle to fall asleep, stay asleep or both. You might dream more or less than you normally do. You might have good dreams, or you might have nightmares.

Sleep is really important — especially when you are grieving — because being well rested can make the grief experience a little less difficult. When you sleep, your body repairs and restores itself. While you are grieving, you are under more stress than normal, so it makes sense that you'll need more sleep each night. Your body might need more time at night to repair itself because your days are more intense and draining than normal.

You probably don't even realize how much sleep (or a lack of it) affects you. When people regularly don't get enough sleep they might feel kind of blah, like everything takes more effort than usual. Sometimes it can feel like you're getting sick. Or maybe you get angry a lot more quickly, and you lose your temper over things that wouldn't normally upset you. You might be kind of mean to friends or family and not even realize it. You might not be able to focus in class, so you do poorly on a test or on your homework. A lack of sleep can really wreck your life. That's why it's so important to pay attention to your sleep habits during this time.

So what can you do? It might sound basic (and be annoying to read) but avoiding phones and electronics in bed can make a big difference. Instead, switch to reading a physical book or an e-reader — the point is to avoid bright screens and endless scrolling. You could also try going to bed a little earlier. Just by getting enough sleep, you can reduce other physical, cognitive and emotional signs associated with grief.

As with sleep, you might find you need to drink more water than normal, so make sure you're drinking enough throughout the day. Otherwise, you will feel sluggish and have headaches.

Another example of a behavioral sign would be changes in your eating habits. Many people, while grieving, eat more than normal. Others don't have much of an appetite at all.

You also might notice changes in how you behave at school or with your friends. You might notice yourself picking fights, acting out or otherwise just not being yourself.

When it comes to your behavior while grieving, it makes sense that you might not act like yourself. Who would? Look at everything that can pile up: lots of stress from dealing with the loss, not getting enough sleep, not eating enough and maybe your daily routine at home has totally changed. Of course you aren't yourself!

These changes are normal and, with time, will either fade away or go back to what was usual before the loss.

Sometimes our behaviors can negatively affect other people though, and we don't want to dump our pain on someone else who doesn't deserve it. Your brain might say, "Fill up the emptiness!" ("Eat!") or "Get this hurt out!" ("Hurt someone else and give it to them!"). These solutions won't actually help in the long run, but it's normal to "act first, think later" when stressed.

SOCIAL SiGNS

When people are experiencing grief,
they might want to be by themselves
and not hang out with their friends or
family at all. Other people might want
to go out every night and have people
around them all the time. Grief can change
social butterflies into lone wolves and vice versa.

It's hard to change when people already have a set idea of
you, especially when they're your friends. Though teens and
tweens — even adults! — change all the time, members of
social groups feel more secure when they know everyone's
roles and identities. If the class clown is suddenly serious
all the time, his classmates might lash out and say, "What's
wrong with him?" If they thought about it, most would
understand that he shouldn't be expected to be the joker
forever, but that strong desire to have everything be familiar
makes it hard to accept changes in other people.

You can tell your friends that you know you aren't feeling
like yourself right now because you are grieving. You can
also tell them how to support you. If you want to be invited
out more because it helps you feel better, tell them. Or, if
you don't want to hang out but aren't sure how long that

will last, tell them to keep inviting you to do things — even though you might say no, the invitation helps you feel better. Remember that it is always okay to say you are grieving and you don't really know what you need right now!

EMOTiONAL SIGNS

Finally! We get to emotions. Sadness and anger are the feelings most associated with grieving, but did you know joy, excitement and confusion can be part of grief, too? *Any* feeling can be part of grieving — even happiness.

An important thing to know about emotional signs is that when you are grieving, you might feel *more* emotional than normal or *less* emotional.

Some people do not cry after a loved one dies. Some people might cry after one loss but not after another. This might make them think something is wrong with them or that it's a sign they didn't really love that person. But it might be simply that their grief isn't showing through emotional signs. Maybe they have more physical signs or cognitive signs. Not everyone cries, and that is okay.

ALEJANDRO

Rubí, a beagle, had been in Alejandro's life for as long as he could remember. Rubí was very small, and one of her eyes would drift slightly to one side. She had very soft ears and the tip of her tail was bright white. When she died, Alejandro was devastated. She wasn't there to jump into his arms after school. She wasn't there to sit on his lap when he did his homework or to sleep on his feet every night. In the first few weeks after Rubí died, Alejandro's grief was sharp. He would instantly cry in the morning because she wasn't there. When he realized he was standing at the back door, Alejandro would start to cry again. Without even thinking, he had walked over to let her out to go pee.

It was yet another reminder that she was gone. It seemed like there were dozens of these reminders every day. Rubí's absence was just as strong as her presence in his life when she was alive.

After the first month, Alejandro noticed that he wasn't crying every morning. He still cried, but it felt like an ache instead of a tear in his heart. He could think about happy times with Rubí and how funny she was and smile instead of cry.

Alejandro's mom printed a picture of him and Rubí. He picked out a wood frame because Rubí liked to bring sticks from the yard into the house sometimes, and he thought she would like it. Alejandro put the framed photo next to his bed. Seeing her every morning when he woke up and every night before bed brought him comfort.

ANTICIPATORY GRIEF

There's a kind of grief that shows up *before* a deathloss (Chapter Two) or a shadowloss (Chapter Three). ⌠Anticipatory grief⌡ commonly appears when you find out a loved one has an illness or injury they will die from, but they haven't yet. The grief you are experiencing comes from the loss you know will happen in the future, even if you don't know precisely when. You anticipate (expect) it will happen and are grieving already. Grieving before someone dies doesn't mean you can't also enjoy the time you have left together — you can do both at once. It can feel weird to navigate saying goodbye while also creating new memories.

You can also experience anticipatory grief with a shadowloss. For example, maybe your older sibling will be moving away to college this summer, or you find out you'll have to switch schools next year. Many people said they noticed more anger and anxiety with anticipatory grief than after a deathloss. Every anticipatory grief experience is unique to you and the expected loss, and it is normal for the grief *before* a loss to be different than the grief *after* a loss.

ALL GRiEF IS NORMAL GRiEF

Throughout this book, you will see all kinds of thoughts, feelings and behaviors associated with grief described as "normal." It can be helpful to hear that what you are feeling and experiencing has been felt and experienced by others before. But the truth is, there really is no such thing as "normal" grief because all expressions of grief can be normal. There is only *your* grief.

Your grief is as unique as you and the loss you've experienced. And because every loss is unique, you may never grieve the same way twice. What's also tricky is that as you get older, the way you grieve can change.

When you grieve at eight years old, you might cry most of the day and feel tired all the time. But maybe, at 15 years old, you won't cry as much, but you notice you can't focus or get anything done.

Part of taking care of yourself through your grief process is understanding that there is no "right" or "wrong" way to grieve. You can't control it — how you grieve is how you grieve.

This applies to your friends and family, too. They might be grieving in a totally different way than you, but you never want to try to change the way someone else grieves — you can't; you simply have to accept their way as being different and not better or worse.

Grief is a process that presents different challenges from day to day and changes with each person as they grow and change throughout their entire life. That is why it is so important to listen to your body. By paying attention to how you are affected by grief, you'll be better able to support yourself through the grieving process.

So now you know what grief can look and feel like. But when does the grief process start? Well, it always begins with an ending.

Carry this with you

1. Grief is not a feeling. It is a process. Grief is how we respond to loss.

2. Signs of a grief response can be grouped into six categories: cognitive, physical, spiritual, behavioral, social and emotional.

3. Get plenty of sleep and drink lots of water.

4. Not everyone cries.

5. Anticipatory grief is grief that happens before an expected deathloss or a shadowloss.

6. Your expression of grief is as unique as you are.

A RAINBOW OF GRATITUDE

Storms don't last forever. Rainbows often show up at the end of a storm, reminding us that sunny days are ahead.

Have you ever seen a rainbow when there are still dark clouds in the sky? Or even when you can still hear thunder? The rainbow on this page does not mean you should ignore the storms in your life; it is here to remind you of the sunny days ahead. Get your journal or a piece of paper and sketch out a rainbow like the example on the next page. On each band of the rainbow, write the name of a person or animal you are grateful for, or write a short sentence about something you are grateful for.

When you are grieving, even the teeniest tiniest things count. Your favorite pair of shoes might be something you appreciate these days because they feel comfortable and familiar. Or maybe you're thankful for your school counselor, who you feel like you can really talk to.

my cozy room

♥ •ROO + PEACHO•

The bench at the top of Sixth Lookout

Holly + Anna P + Ewa + Siobhan + Jenny ☺

LiCORiCe   mom's old camera 📷

The manga section at Mainlanders

my headphones 🎧 → GREG ←

SOPHIE, SAM & KALEIGH ♥

Chapter Two

DEATHLOSS

Has someone you cared about died? When you lose an important person in your life, it is painful and overwhelming. Now you are grieving their loss. This is really hard.

Before you read this chapter, imagine a flickering candle, say the name of your special someone and give yourself a hug.

In this chapter, you will learn what a deathloss is, the two things that usually come with a deathloss and the two things that deathlosses are not.

Loving Kindness

I will be patient with myself.

WHAT iS A "DEATHLOSS"?

A deathloss occurs when a person or animal we love dies. It's called a deathloss because the physical world changes — someone who was alive and moving around and doing things is no longer. Maybe your pet is no longer asking to go outside or snoring at the bottom of your bed. You feel their absence. Or your grandpa died, and you no longer go to his house on Tuesdays. Perhaps there is now an empty desk at school where your classmate used to sit. Or your brother's bedroom sits empty.

It's a deathloss because the death of a person or animal is a loss. The person or animal that lived in the same world with you at the same time is no longer there. At least, not there in the same way.

WHAT TO EXPECT WiTH A DEATHLOSS

Whenever a deathloss happens in your life, two things usually come along with it: grief and a funeral.

Grief, as you know from Chapter One, is how you uniquely respond to a loss. Grieving can be exhausting and a huge disruption in life. It makes sense why sometimes we might try to ignore or avoid it. But this is impossible. Grieving is as inevitable as puberty. And it's not something you can get "better at" with practice. You might get better at managing the disruption in your life though. For example, the first time you grieve you might keep showing up for basketball practice. You might feel it's more important to go to your friend's birthday party than to listen to your body telling you to rest. The next time you grieve, you will know to cancel everything in the coming weeks. You are getting better at listening to your needs, but you can't get better at "solving" or "getting over" grief because it is not something to solve or get over.

With every deathloss you experience in your life, your grief response will probably change a little each time.

The second thing that happens when there is a deathloss (of a person, at least) is a funeral. A funeral is any ceremony that honors a dead person. Usually that includes what happens to the body, which is called disposition. The two most common kinds of disposition are burial or cremation. Burial means the body is put in the ground (most often in a cemetery), and cremation means the body is put through fire until just the bones remain. At the end of the cremation, the bones are pulverized into a grainy powder. The crushed-up powder is called "cremated remains," but a lot of people call them "ashes." Sometimes people bury the cremated remains, put them into an urn and keep them at home or scatter them in an important place. It can be a comfort to remember that the stuff that makes up your body (and everyone else's) will all stay together in the same spot in the universe, right here on planet Earth. As Carl Sagan, an American astronomer, pointed out in his book *Cosmos*, the elements that make up our bodies — nitrogen, calcium, iron, carbon and so on — were formed inside collapsing stars. We are connected to everything in the universe.

Humans have been saying goodbye to loved ones (humans or animals) as long as we have existed. Most scientists agree humans have been around for about 200 000 years. That means we have been dying for that long, too. Scientists have a theory that a funeral ceremony is a ritual that people developed as a way of coping with the loss of the person in the community. The desire to come together to say goodbye to our loved ones who have died is part of what makes us human. It is natural for us to mourn.

You can also think of a funeral ceremony as medicine — grief medicine. When you are with your family and friends who are also grieving, it can help to see their different signs of grief. You might feel less alone or at least better able to accept that there is no right way to feel or act. It also helps to talk about the person and what they meant to you and listen to others do the same. The funeral is an important step because it will help with healing. It may taste bitter and it might be painful to have to go through it, but ultimately it will help you move forward and find a new normal.

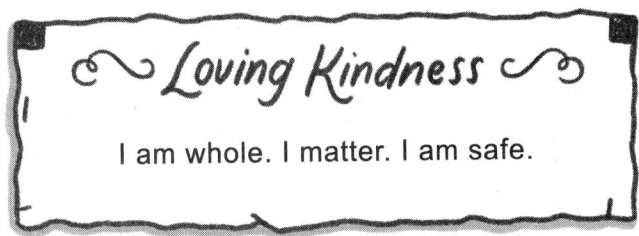

Loving Kindness

I am whole. I matter. I am safe.

JACOB

Before Jacob's mom's friend died of breast cancer, she requested that everyone wear pink to her funeral. Jacob dressed for the funeral in new pink shoes. Their mom wore a bright pink dress with a shiny pink belt and matching high heels. She put a pink ribbon on Jacob's shirt. Jacob felt nervous about all this pink. They were expecting everyone to wear black and be really quiet. When they arrived at the church, Jacob was surprised. They grinned, and then they felt weird for smiling at a funeral. *Everyone* was wearing pink, even the minister. All the flowers were pink. There were pink balloon arrangements. The tables were covered in pink tablecloths. The program with information about the funeral service was neon pink. When their mom signed the guestbook, the pens had pink ink. Jacob was there to support their mom, and they themselves weren't grieving, but they felt cheered up to be a part of something like this. It was like everyone was on the same team, and they could feel a strong sense of community, even though not everyone knew each other.

FUNERALS FOR PEOPLE

While the death of a person — no matter where on Earth — is usually marked by a funeral, it can look and feel very different depending on your religion, culture or family tradition. Some funerals can be very loud. There might be vibrant music, crying, wailing or drumming. There might be laughing. They can also be very quiet with no music at all and little to no crying or visible emotions. Depending on your culture, people attending a funeral might wear all black or all white. And sometimes the family might request everyone dress a certain way or wear something in honor of the person who died.

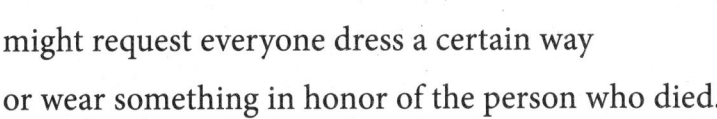

Funerals can be very short, or can last for many days. One group of people, the Hmong, have a funeral ritual that takes place over three days but doesn't completely finish for up to a year. On the first day of the funeral, the family of the dead person spends time with guests who come to visit, they accept gifts and prayers are said. On the second day, traditional offerings are made and rituals with ceremonial items occur. Everyone in attendance eats together. On the third day, the burial happens. A drummer and a qeej player (the instrument, pronounced "geng," is made of bamboo and sounds similar to bagpipes) lead the way to the cemetery. A woman carrying a torch follows behind them. Behind her are all the people attending the funeral. And behind all the attendees is the dead person being carried on a stretcher or in a casket. This funeral ritual has a final act called a Xi.

During a Xi, the family invites the soul of the dead person to visit their home in preparation for its journey into the afterlife. This ritual can happen up to a full year after the person has been buried, and only once that happens is the funeral ritual finally complete.

Funerals can take many forms. One type of funeral that is very common for many Christians and nonreligious families starts with a funeral service and ends with burial. The service might happen outside at the cemetery where the person is to be buried or inside a building (a church, community center, chapel building located at the cemetery or banquet hall). All the mourners gather together and the ceremony begins. Many times, these funeral services start with a song or a reading, and then a more formal story is told about the person who died, which is called a ⌐eulogy⌐. One person often leads the entire funeral service but it is also common for many people to do different parts. After that part of the service, the next step takes place at the cemetery if the person is being buried. Sometimes more words are said at the graveside. Sometimes not. And if the person is being cremated, not buried, there may not be this second part. Many families will gather somewhere to eat after a funeral service and burial, sometimes at someone's house or out at a restaurant. It's normal for funerals to be exhausting — they are often very long days full of tears, feelings of all kinds and wearing nice clothes you don't normally wear.

All funerals have one thing in common: people grieving the dead person come together to acknowledge that loss. Those who are grieving (called mourners) might come together and pray, they might come together to bury the body or they might come together to just sit in silence. Your culture, religion or family tradition will guide you with what to expect.

If you are going to a funeral but aren't sure what to expect, you should ask an adult.

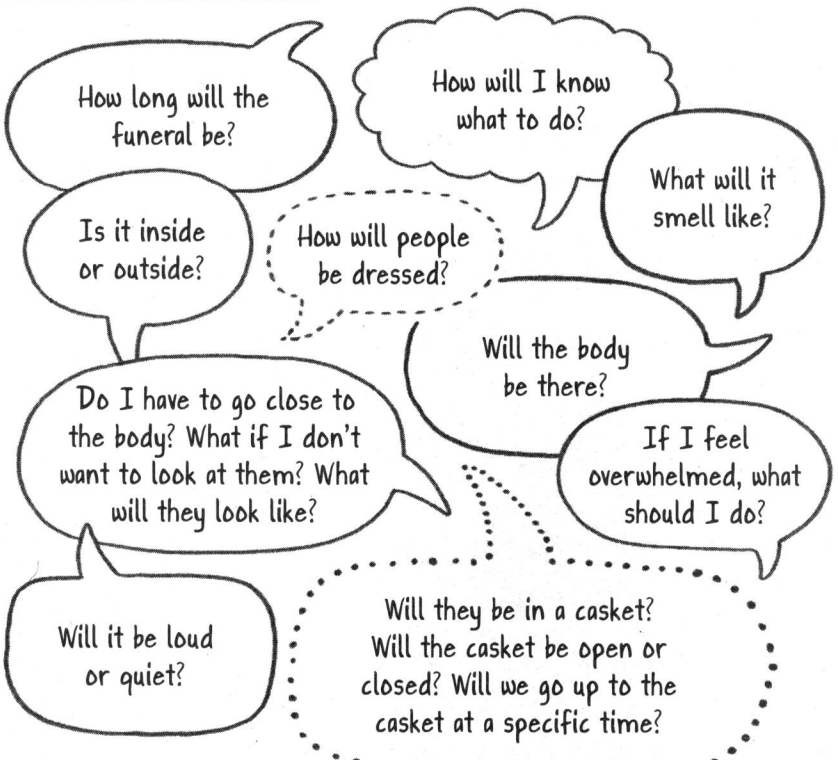

Sometimes, for a variety of reasons, a funeral doesn't happen. A person might ask for no funeral when they die, or a major event (like a pandemic, war or disaster) could

prevent one from taking place. When there is no funeral, it doesn't mean that the person who died was loved any less or any differently. You can always do something to honor your loved one privately — like a very tiny funeral that only you attend. Your tiny funeral for your loved one can happen at home, in your room or anywhere you choose, and no one has to know. A funeral, after all, is just the name we give to a specific time we dedicate to remembering our loved one, and you never need permission to remember someone you love.

FUNERALS FOR ANIMALS

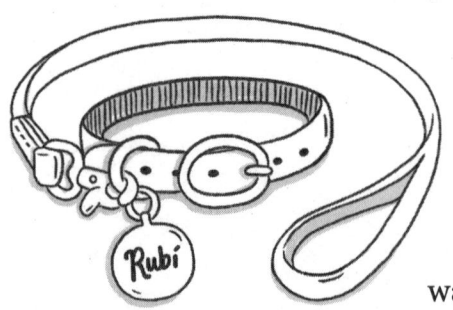

We don't have funerals for animals like we do for people, but your family might still gather in some way to grieve or talk about the loss together. They just might not call it a funeral. It can be hard with pets because we often grieve them just as deeply as we do people, but we don't have the same rituals for pets, such as gathering together to say goodbye. This can feel as though your pet wasn't as important as a person. You might feel you're the only one feeling sad and that can make you feel angry.

But just as it is powerful and healing to gather with other people when a person dies, a funeral for an animal can be important grief medicine. Having a place and time dedicated to talking and thinking about a beloved animal that died might be an important step to take on your grief journey.

ALEJANDRO

When Rubí died, Alejandro's entire family gathered in the backyard to bury her. Everyone took turns digging the hole. Then Alejandro's mom placed flowers in the bottom, and his dad wrapped Rubí's body up in a knitted blanket that Alejandro's abuela had made for her when she was just a puppy. Rubí looked peaceful atop a bed of flowers, wrapped in that cozy and colorful blanket. Alejandro placed her favorite toy, a neon green bone, beside her. Everyone cried and Alejandro's mom sang a song they often sang at church. Everyone took turns saying some final words and Alejandro's dad stayed behind to finish burying Rubí. This was a funeral for Rubí, even though nobody called it that.

WAYS TO HONOR THE DEATH OF A PET

Remembering your pet can be a creative, special and healing experience you do on your own or with your family and friends. Here are a few ideas:

PLACE A PHOTO OR A DRAWING OF YOUR PET IN A SPECIAL PLACE AND KEEP THEIR FAVORITE THINGS NEARBY

TURN YOUR DOG OR CAT'S FAVORITE TOY OR COLLAR INTO A Holiday Ornament BY ATTACHING A STRING OR ORNAMENT HOOK

PLANT A TREE OR A FLOWER IN MEMORY OF YOUR PET

KEEP A SNIPPET OF YOUR PET'S FUR IN A LOCKET

ASK A PARENT OR GUARDIAN IF YOU OR YOUR FAMILY CAN MAKE A DONATION TO A LOCAL ZOO OR ANIMAL SHELTER IN YOUR PET'S NAME

WHAT ISN'T A DEATHLOSS

Now that you know about two things that usually come with a deathloss, you should know about two things that are not part of deathlosses.

When you hear that someone you didn't know has died, you might feel sad and you might think about it for a while, but it isn't a deathloss for you. Let's say you are in the middle of class when your teacher is called to the office. After a few minutes, the principal arrives to tell the class that your teacher's dad has died and your teacher won't be returning for a few days. You never met your teacher's dad.

You might not even know his name. But you might be sad for your teacher. It can feel really intense when something like this happens — you might even cry yourself. Your feelings are coming from a place of care and concern for your teacher and that is totally normal. We never want to see people we like in pain, so it makes sense that we might have an emotional reaction when we do see that.

Loving Kindness

This won't last forever.

DIYA

Diya's grandfather died last year. She didn't really know him because he lived over a thousand miles away on the other side of India. When he died, Diya didn't really feel sad. She didn't feel a sense of loss, since he wasn't really a part of her life. Sure, she knew stories about him, and she knew that he knew a little about what was going on in her life, but they didn't have much of a connection. Diya's grandfather's death wasn't a deathloss for her. But Diya's cousin, Bhavi, had a very different experience when their grandfather died. She lived in the same house with him, so he was a very large part of her life. After he died, Bhavi felt her grandfather's absence every day. She experienced his death as a deathloss.

What's important to know is that while your teacher had a deathloss, you did not. You could tell your teacher that you are sad for their loss, but you do not need to feel like you should be sadder than you actually are. If you didn't know the person who died, it's okay to not grieve them. Just like you can't skip grieving when you experience a deathloss, you also can't force yourself to grieve when you haven't actually had one. A deathloss is not something other people get to decide for you.

Your grief experience is your own. Grief can look very different from person to person, even if you are experiencing the same loss, and even if you are in the same family. This is normal and okay. Part of the experience of grief is making space for everyone to be exactly as they are.

When somebody says they need to "make space" for grief, they mean they want to make sure it doesn't get ignored or swept under the rug. Many adults (and kids!) struggle with "taking up space." Have you ever been out with your friends at the mall and everyone but you wants to go to a specific store? And because you don't want to inconvenience anyone or because your friends aren't interested in the same kind of stores that you are, you just don't say anything at all and go along with what everyone else wants? It's kind of like that. Making space for yourself means that when you have a need, a want or a desire, you will ask for it or share it with others. It means you won't tell yourself no just because you think the people around you might say no.

When it comes to grief, we can sometimes feel self-conscious about our needs. Grief isn't something that disappears after 24 hours. In a way, it is something that will always be with you. You will go through periods of time when you notice your grief signs more than others, and you will probably have higher needs as a result. Other times, entire weeks will go by before you realize that you haven't really noticed any grief signs at all! That's okay and that's normal. Just remember that you deserve to take up space; your feelings are real and valid, and when you make space for yourself, you're showing love to yourself.

GRiEVING PEOPLE YOU DIDN'T KNOW

Have you ever grieved the loss of someone you didn't know in real life — and who wasn't even connected to anyone you knew — but you *felt* like you knew them? It is possible to grieve the death of a movie star, musician, athlete, social media star or other public figure. While you may not have known them in real life, they were still a part of your life. In some ways, you might have more of a connection to certain celebrities, movie stars, social media creators or musicians than some people you know in real life. You might feel closer to these creators because you interact with what they create so often. Maybe you watch your favorite YouTuber twice a week, listen to your favorite singer every morning and watch (and rewatch) your favorite actor's movies every weekend. You might have saved your favorite influencer's videos to your phone. These are real people, and their presence — through their art or their activities — is real in your life. When you think about it that way, you can see why you might deeply feel the loss of someone you've never even met before.

When NBA player Kobe Bryant died in January 2020, it was a deathloss for a lot of his fans. Many people cried. They posted on social media about how sad they were that he died; they talked with other people who likely didn't know Kobe Bryant in real life but were also mourning him. These fans had posters of him on their bedroom walls. They'd watched him play basketball, cheering him on from their homes or in stadiums. They'd followed his career and his life. When he died, it was a shared loss. A part of many people's lives — someone they talked about with friends, and someone who was a part of our culture — died.

EMMA

Emma's mom died just after the start of the school year. At first, Emma felt like she would never stop crying. She loved her mom. She looked up to her. Emma's favorite subject in school was science because her mom was a biologist, and she wanted to be just like her.

The week Emma returned to school after her mother's funeral, the theme of that year's science fair was announced. Every year since fourth grade, her mom would help her with her science fair project. It was one of Emma's favorite parts of the school year. But there would be no more late nights together designing experiments. They wouldn't laugh together over messy failed attempts. The more Emma thought about what she'd lost, she became angry. She couldn't remember having ever been this angry at her mom when she was alive. She felt like her mom had abandoned her and stolen a lifetime of memories.

For the next several weeks, Emma would come home from school each day and go straight to her room. She'd hide there because she didn't want anyone else to see her like this, but also because she wanted to be alone with all her anger. It made her feel her mom's presence in the burning in her chest.

Eventually though, holding on to all of that fire became too exhausting. One afternoon, after coming home from a long day at school, Emma went to her room and lay on her bed like she had been doing every day since the funeral. But this time was a little different. She was too tired to be angry, she had no tears left to cry, and a tiny moment of quiet drifted into her mind. She thought about what her mom would say to her in that moment, and the memory of her mother's voice and encouragement melted away all the anger she'd been holding.

YOUR RELATIONSHIP WILL CONTINUE

There's one more thing you should know about deathlosses. Just because a person or animal you love dies doesn't mean your relationship stops existing. In the future, when your grandparents die, you will still continue to love them many years later. In the same way, you will still fondly remember your childhood pet 20 years from now. I hope it is comforting to know your relationship with that person or animal will continue to develop and change as time goes by.

With any deathloss, it's important to know that it's okay to still love that person, or to still be angry sometimes with that person, or to feel any way you felt about them when they were alive. Anything you can feel about a living person you can feel about someone who is dead. Their body died, but your relationship did not. It just changed. And it will continue on.

BIG QUESTIONS AFTER A DEATHLOSS

When there is a deathloss in your life, you will inevitably ask yourself two questions: "Why did they die?" and "Will I die, too?"

Ask *What*, Not *Why*

"Why did they die?" can be a tricky question because the answer doesn't always make us feel better. All people will die eventually, and the things that cause them to die can be as simple as old age or something more complicated. It can be hard to find a satisfying answer to a lot of "why" questions. Why are we alive? Why does the sun exist? Why, why, why? It can be useful to ask "what" questions instead. Sometimes those questions can provide us with answers that help us keep our grief moving. Questions like "What can I do to honor their memory?" or "What would they say to me right now?" or "What would they want me to do?" can connect us to meaningful understanding about our loved ones ... and ourselves.

When Wishes Definitely Don't Come True

After someone dies it is very common for people to worry that they somehow caused it. Have you ever become angry at someone and yelled "I WISH YOU WERE DEAD!"? Well, that happens to a lot of us as we grow up, but it is definitely *never* something that would actually cause someone to die. That's the honest truth. Kids have been yelling that at parents, siblings, friends and teachers for centuries — it's something we might look back on and feel bad about, but that's it.

Will I Die, Too?

You are going to die one day. But you won't die because someone you love died, even though it might feel that way. That is the very special thing that connects you to me, and connects you to every single person who ever lived, and every single animal that ever lived, and every single plant that ever lived. They all had (or will have) this same experience. Death. Also birth! All people, animals and plants have a start date (and an end date) here on Earth.

Even furniture "dies." Have you ever had a piece of furniture in your home that broke and you had to get rid of it? Well, technically, that piece of furniture had a start date — the day it was made. And it also has an end date — the day it "died."

As we learned in Chapter One, many adults kind of freak out about death. They are afraid that by talking to young people about death, they will really upset them or make them cry. And they are also afraid to face the upsetting feelings that might come up when they talk about death — anxiety thinking of their own death or their loved ones dying or sadness remembering someone's death from long ago. It sucks. It's hard. It's sad.

But it is normal. It's part of the human experience — one of the hardest parts.

Since we know we all will die at some point, it's important to love yourself and to love your life.

So get started now! Life is too special not to love yourself and not to love your life. Start with finding the tiny, ordinary things you love about your life, and about yourself, and celebrate them.

It's more important to focus on your life, which has so much within it you get to make decisions about, versus your death, which is something you don't get to decide. Your life is a complex, deep experience and death is just an event. As you get older, you will see how important it is to live your life the way you want. Focusing on death keeps you completely stuck — and can stop you from living your life.

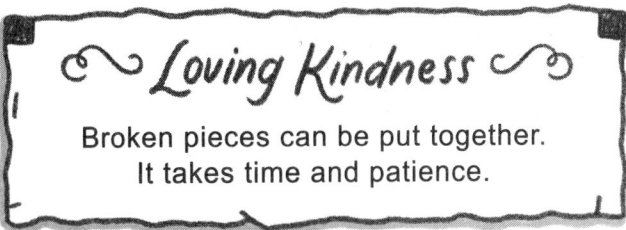

~ *Loving Kindness* ~

Broken pieces can be put together.
It takes time and patience.

Carry this with you

1. A deathloss happens when a person or animal we love dies.

2. Funerals are like medicine for our grief. They help grievers connect and find support in one another. Funerals also help us to move forward with our grief and find a new normal.

3. There are many different ways to hold a funeral. Funeral rituals are guided by culture, religion and family traditions.

4. Everyone (and everything) eventually dies. Don't get stuck by focusing on death. Focus on life.

LIGHTING A CANDLE

People will come to know the person who died through the people they had an impact on. In that way, a part of the people we love so much will always live on in us. If you learned how to cook from someone who died, and you teach someone else to cook, you are passing on that lesson from your loved one.

Get your journal or a piece of paper and sketch out some candles like the example on the next page. When you think of your loved one, what did they teach you? What is something you appreciate or enjoy because of them? What's a story about them you will never forget? Write these things below each candle and you will see how their light will continue to shine on in you.

Chapter Three

SHADOWLOSS

There is another kind of loss that doesn't involve the death of a person or animal. And the grief response your mind and body feels can be just as overwhelming as the grief from a deathloss. This is called a shadowloss. Just as everyone experiences grief and deathlosses in their lifetime, everyone will experience a shadowloss. In fact, shadowlosses are more common than deathlosses.

WHAT iS A "SHADOWLOSS"?

While a deathloss is a loss *of* life, a shadowloss is a loss *in* life. To put it another way, a deathloss is the death of some*one* while a shadowloss is the death of some*thing*. And even though they can sometimes be harder to recognize

(because there is no dead body to show for it), shadowlosses can be just as devastating as deathlosses. The end — in other words, the death — of a thing in your life has very real and lasting effects.

What Are Some Examples of a Shadowloss?

Shadowlosses can take many forms, and what is a shadowloss for you may not be one for someone else. This list shows a few common examples of shadowlosses. If you don't see your shadowloss listed, that doesn't mean it's not real.

- ☐ Changing schools
- ☐ Losing a big opportunity, like an audition or a spot on a team
- ☐ Moving to a new town
- ☐ Divorce
- ☐ Getting ghosted or a friendship ending
- ☐ A medical diagnosis, like cancer, celiac disease or ADHD
- ☐ A pandemic
- ☐ A war
- ☐ A natural disaster
- ☐ A school shooting or mass shooting
- ☐ Puberty

In these examples, maybe no one close to you died, but some*thing* was lost — the way things were, the hopes for a certain kind of future, the idea of who you are.

Let's take divorce, for example. A divorce is the death of a marriage. For some people, a divorce might feel like the death of their family as they knew it or expected it to be. You still have a family after a divorce, but it might be different than what you thought it would be like.

There's also something called "ghosting" that many people experience as a shadowloss. Ghosting happens when someone, often a friend, stops responding to you completely. Usually, you don't know why this happens. They don't reply to texts, they might unfriend you on social media — it's almost like they died … except they are still alive. In a way, they become a ghost in your life. Many people grieve this shadowloss because some*thing* died (the friendship or the future you would have shared together), not some*one*. Even though the person didn't die, you have lost that person's presence in your life.

Another example of a shadowloss is the COVID-19 pandemic. For many people, the pandemic meant the death of what was "normal." Our daily routines, traditions and sense of safety in the world "died." Did you miss out on a vacation or lose touch with friends because of the pandemic?

Many of you could not go to parks or malls as usual. Sports and music lessons stopped. Suddenly, everyone was wearing masks everywhere they went. So much changed and so much was lost. Normal died.

The pandemic brought many deathlosses with it. Not only did many people die from COVID-19, but many other people and animals died — from other causes — yet the rituals of funerals and the usual supports and comforts (going to school to talk things over with friends, going to religious services or visiting grandparents) were not there for us. It was a time of loss upon loss, and you might still be reeling from the shock of losing so much at once.

Getting diagnosed with a medical condition or illness can also be a shadowloss. Finding out you have cancer, for example, can feel like the death of you being healthy and the idea of you as someone who never had a serious illness. Even when you recover, you will never *not* have had cancer. And you might have missed out on experiences and opportunities while you were sick.

BAO

Bao and her sister had to move across town with their mother when their parents divorced. They had to go to a new school and live in a new apartment in a new neighborhood. They shopped at a different grocery store, and they didn't see their old friends from their old neighborhood very often, if at all. For Bao, this move and everything that came with it was a shadowloss. While no one actually died, Bao grieved because everything that was normal for her had, in a sense, died. On the other hand, Bao's sister did not experience the move the same way. The move made things better for her in many ways. She was bullied at her old school, so the move meant she could get away from all of that and start fresh. For her, even though she was sad that her parents got divorced, she didn't grieve all the changes. It wasn't a shadowloss for her.

Something really important to understand about a shadowloss is that two different people can experience the same kind of event (such as a divorce or moving to a new city) but only one person might feel it's a shadowloss.

In the same way that other people can't decide for you what is or isn't a deathloss, they also can't tell you when you have or have not experienced a shadowloss. Only you and your own feelings and emotions can tell you when you've suffered one. A shadowloss is something we claim for ourselves.

GRiEVING SHADOWLOSSES

Many people, even adults, don't
know that it's possible to grieve
some*thing* that dies. That's what
makes a shadowloss so tricky;
we don't always see it happening
in ourselves, and we definitely
don't always see it happening to others.

But just like with deathlosses, we can grieve and mourn
our shadowlosses. There are a few differences between
the two that can be helpful to know.

It is normal, healthy and expected to have some kind of
funeral when a person or animal we love dies. But there
aren't funerals for divorces, changing schools or the end of a
friendship. However, we still can grieve those things just as
hard as — or harder than — we grieve the loss of a loved one.

Funerals give us a place to express and hold our grief. It's
a time and place for mourners to show up and share in the
loss together. It's a time and a place where it's okay for others
to see your sadness and tears. With a shadowloss, we don't
have that — there is no time and place to show up and be
sad together like we get with a deathloss.

BAO

When Bao's parents divorced, it sure felt like there had been a death. But while her parents' divorce was a fact everyone knew about, nobody talked about it.

Bao felt like she couldn't talk to anyone about it. The divorce was the hardest thing she had ever been through, and it was still hard almost every day after. It was like the family itself had died. Her parents had their own separate lives now, and she had two different bedrooms. Every time she was at one house, she needed something left at the other. Nothing was right, and nothing felt like home.

Bao sometimes told herself she shouldn't be so upset. Lots of kids at school had parents who were divorced.

But, in reality, Bao's life had been just as impacted by her parents' divorce, if not more, than any deathloss she had ever experienced. Every aspect of her life changed because of the divorce, and there were so many things she had to say goodbye to. The divorce was a shadowloss for Bao. Someone didn't die, but something did — in fact, so many things died — her parents' marriage, her family and home as she knew them, and celebrating holidays together. Not literally, of course, but so many things stopped existing the way they had. She sometimes felt like she was grieving a thousand things because of the divorce, and each day she would discover something else that would never again be the same.

Without this public way of marking a loss, it is very easy to ignore or overlook that you are grieving. You might think, "Why are you so upset? It's not like somebody died!" And while that is true, no*body* died, some*thing* did, and that is no less important. With shadowloss, people very often grieve but feel they have to hide it from others.

When you have a shadowloss, other people might not be the only ones who don't take it seriously. Like Bao, you might also think it shouldn't be such a big deal. But as with a deathloss, your body and your brain will be stressed, and they will put out lots of signs. Unlike with a deathloss though, people — including you — might not be looking out for these signs.

You know from Chapter One that grief is not something we can control. It is just how we respond to loss. That loss might be of a person or animal, or it might be the loss of the way things were. We don't get to choose what or how or when we grieve. It doesn't matter if your grief is the result of a deathloss or a shadowloss — grief is grief.

ᴄ∿ *Loving Kindness* ᴄ∿

I believe I can heal.

You might be relieved to now know why you've been feeling the way you do. Maybe you've been sad or tired all the time, or you've been experiencing ups and downs and your emotions being all over the place. You can now say, "I am grieving." But now what? Everyone seems to want you to "get over it," but how do you do that? Can you even get over it? Grief is a process. The next few chapters describe helpful tools to work through it.

BE KIND.
I'M GRIEVING
BE GENTLE.

Carry this with you

1. A deathloss is a loss of life. A shadowloss is a loss in life.

2. People grieve shadowlosses the same way they grieve deathlosses.

3. Only you can identify what is and is not a shadowloss in your life.

4. What a shadowloss is for one person may not be for another — even from the same event.

A SACRED SPOT

Though the impact of a shadowloss can be just as large, if not larger, on you than a deathloss, it can be harder to process that impact without physical rituals of grief. It might feel good for you to acknowledge your shadowloss in a more physical way, since we don't have funerals for shadowlosses like we do when a loved one dies.

Choose a sacred spot in your room, your home or any place that is meaningful to you. You can choose a spot inside a desk drawer or on a bookshelf. In this spot, put three to five physical things that remind you of your shadowloss. If you had to move away, maybe it's a picture of your old house. You can also put things in this special spot that make sense to you but not another person.

If you don't have a physical space to do this, you can do it in your journal or a piece of paper. Draw a shelf and sketch in the items you'd put there. You can also write words if you don't have any ideas for physical objects. Sometimes it's easier to write than it is to draw, so use this space to represent your loss in any way you want.

When you're done, you will have a special place you can visit anytime you want to remember your shadowloss, be present to yourself or connect with something significant that happened to you.

Chapter Four

GRiEF ENERGY

Now that you know what grief is (and isn't), and that people grieve both deathlosses and shadowlosses, it's time to talk about what it feels like. This is called grief energy.

Remember, grief is not something you can turn on or off, and it's not something you can speed up or slow down. It's just part of being human, and it's a normal part of life.

The very first time you grieve, you might feel really uncomfortable. You might feel like something is wrong with you, that maybe you're sick. The first time you grieve, these feelings and sensations inside you can feel weird and unfamiliar.

It *is* weird. It's never happened to you before! It's brand new to you. You haven't had practice with it yet.

Grief is never easy, but you can get better at moving forward with it. The older you get, the more experience you will have grieving. By the time you are 30, you will likely have lost 5–10 people. By the time you are 70, you will have lost 40 or more people. This is a normal part of growing up and getting older.

So, if you are grieving for the first time, remember that as time goes on, it will feel more natural and more familiar to you. Each time it happens, you will get better at knowing what you need and when you need it. You will get better at being there for yourself and others.

WHAT iS GRiEF ENERGY?

When you are grieving, it's normal to feel different types of energy within yourself. You might feel stuck or still, like you don't have any energy to move. You might sit on the couch all day and stare off into space or lie in bed until 3 p.m. Or you might feel like you can't sit down, like you have to keep moving constantly. You might feel one way the first time you grieve and then the exact opposite the next time.

All of this is normal.

The way our grief energy shows up can help us figure out what we need.

If you are very tired and have no energy, then you probably need to rest. If you are very antsy and just want to keep busy, then you probably need to be more active.

The key is to make sure you are supporting what you need in a healthy way. There are ways to be active that are healthier than others, just like there are healthier ways to rest.

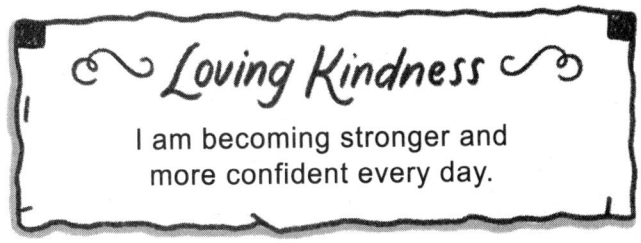

ᴄ⌘ *Loving Kindness* ⌘ᴄ

I am becoming stronger and
more confident every day.

Let's say you are very tired one day and you sleep in late, and then you move to the couch. 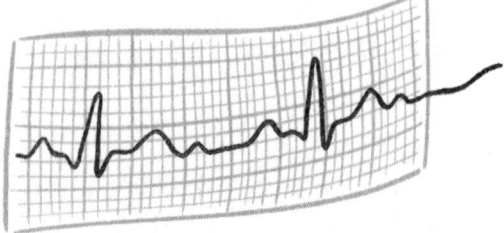 Instead of scrolling through social media on your phone or tablet for six hours, you read a book. Reading keeps your mind engaged but not overwhelmed; with social media, you'll often have strong emotional reactions when you see the carefully presented images of your peers. Seeing your friends laughing together or having incredible experiences with their family can be a reminder of the things you are not doing. Seeing them playing sports, doing funny dances or modeling cool clothes — anything that shows their energy does not match yours — can feel isolating. It can be a tricky thing to learn, but just because you're not running a marathon doesn't mean that you're actually resting. If your body is asking for rest, then your brain probably needs it, too. So the next time you're feeling depleted, don't just rest your body — find something that also quiets your mind, slows your heart rate and makes you feel safe and at ease.

Or imagine you are very antsy — you can't sit still, you click a pen over and over or you're wiggling your foot back and forth. You could bounce around the house interrupting your dad's housework and your sister's guitar practice, or you could take a yoga class on YouTube, go for a long run or shoot hoops in the driveway. Sometimes when we are very antsy — when our pent-up energy wants out — we focus on other people rather than focusing on ourselves and what we need.

Grief energy is a sign of grief, but it can distract us from pain or from uncomfortable feelings. The waves of low or high energy can overwhelm us, and we deal with that one specific sign instead of the grief.

Instead of feeling the sadness and thinking and talking about our loss, it's easier to stay super busy and not sit down and rest. You trick yourself into thinking you're staying ahead of the grief. Instead of feeling how angry you are, it's easier to sleep all day or stare at your phone. You trick yourself into thinking you are fine since you are sleeping through the tough feelings.

When you are grieving, pay attention to what kind of grief energy you have and make sure you aren't avoiding your feelings. Sometimes all that grief energy is our body talking to us: "Hey! These feelings are weird! Let's distract ourselves from it! Let's avoid it!"

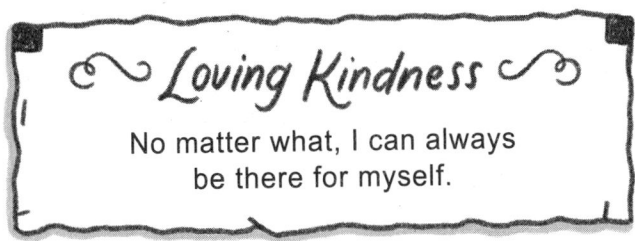

Loving Kindness

No matter what, I can always
be there for myself.

EMMA

Emma has been really angry since her mom died. She has learned that, for her, anger feels like a hot tightness in her chest. They used to try to ignore the feeling of anger by watching funny TikToks, but that feeling would still be there when they turned off their phone. Emma learned that if she put her phone down, she could feel the feeling more fully by noticing how it existed in her body. They felt like the anger was in the front of their chest, almost up to their neck, but not all the way through to their back. Emma would breathe deep breaths in and out, sometimes with tears and sometimes not, and try to figure out where the anger was coming from. Emma thought about her day. They'd been feeling fine when they woke up. Then Emma remembered they had seen a friend walking to school with his mom and his dog. They realized they would never get to go on a walk with their mom and their dog again. They were angry that this was taken from them.

As soon as Emma made the connection between the feeling in her chest and the thing that happened that morning, she noticed the heat in her chest subside and the tightness release. Emma took a big deep breath and exhaled out her mouth, feeling lighter.

When you pay attention to what you are really feeling, you are processing what happened, even if you aren't thinking directly about it. You are also processing the feelings attached to what happened. If you ignore your anger, you won't get the chance to listen to what it's saying or have the opportunity to give it what it needs so it can go away. When we ignore things, we sometimes keep them around. If we just spend a little time with that feeling, we can release it. But you can't release what you aren't willing to first hold.

When you spend time with a feeling, no matter what it is, you might actually feel this sensation in your body.

Emma likely wouldn't have figured out her feeling of anger — processed it — if she hadn't paid attention to her grief energy. It might be similar for you, or maybe it will be a little different. You won't know until you try!

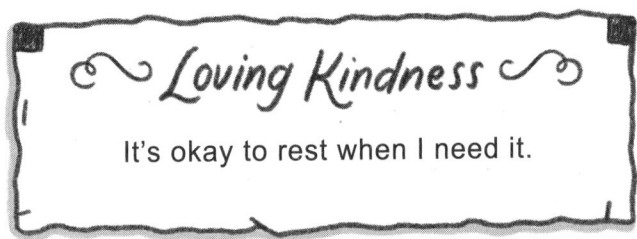

cx Loving Kindness cx

It's okay to rest when I need it.

KEEP YOUR GRiEF MOVING

Grief energy and the pain lying underneath can feel paralyzing. People who are grieving often say they feel stuck. It might feel like you will never feel okay again. It is important to keep your grief moving.

In Emma's story, anger was a part of their grieving process. She kept her grief moving by fully feeling her anger. Doing this helped that feeling transform and dissipate. Emma did this in a healthy way, not trying to ignore it, avoid it or numb it by consuming too much social media. It's normal for people to have different ways of keeping their grief moving in healthy ways, and it does take some trial and error to find what works best for you.

For some people, keeping their grief moving in a healthy way might mean they draw or bake. For others, it might be running.

It took Emma a while before they learned how to feel their feelings and what that process meant for them. Right after their mom died, they were so overwhelmed with strong emotions that all they could do was just stare at their phone and watch TikToks. Doing that seemed to make them notice those feelings less. It distracted them, and they could avoid all those intense feelings. Because all the adults in their life were distracted with what happened to their mom, entire days would go by where Emma was glued to their phone all the times they weren't in school.

EXTRA HELP

CALL OR TEXT 988 IF YOU NEED SOMEONE TO TALK TO AND ARE IN THE UNITED STATES OR CANADA. THERE IS SOMEONE THERE FOR YOU 24/7.

It wasn't until they started going to a grief support group for kids their age that they learned they were doing that to avoid their uncomfortable feelings. Sometimes scrolling was okay if they just needed a break, but doing that for hours on end, or every day or as the only thing they did, kept them stuck in their grief. She wasn't letting herself feel much of anything, and so she wasn't giving herself the chance to move on. The counselors at the support group taught Emma and all the other kids how to feel their feelings, and Emma could feel the anger and sadness and confusion in waves. Sometimes she let the feelings wash over her, forceful and unfamiliar. Sometimes she carried them with her through her day, talking and laughing with classmates but still feeling angry and sad and confused in a quiet part of herself. And sometimes she took a break and ignored it all.

But, for the first time, she was keeping her grief moving. At last, that phrase made sense for her. Distracting themself from their grief was only temporarily holding off all the feelings they needed to feel and things they needed to process.

Another way to think about grief is to picture it as a seed.

Imagine that your grief is a seed that you are given after a deathloss or a shadowloss. This grief seed has the potential to grow and bloom into something new. You get two choices with this grief seed: you can bury it inside yourself, or you can plant it inside yourself. Burying and planting are two very different things. When you plant a seed, you are not only giving it soil, water and sunlight — things it needs to grow — you are also planting hope. Hope that it will grow. And hope that you can be patient enough to wait for it to grow and be able to give it the support that it needs to grow.

But, unless that seed gets water, sunlight and soil, absolutely nothing will change. It will stay exactly how it is, not growing or transforming. In fact, if you just bury a seed and ignore it, it might rot.

Your grief is like this. When you choose to plant your grief seed, it means that you hope it will grow and bloom into something new. The seed itself will always be there, just like the deathloss or shadowloss that caused your grief. It will always be a part of you. Keeping your grief moving means you will make the effort to nurture your grief seed.

Emma first chose to bury their grief seed. The soil they used to cover it up took the form of scrolling through social media for hours, zoning out and trying to distract themself from any negative or intense feelings. After she learned new skills at the grief support group, she decided to plant her seed. Now she looks for any new signs and tries new ways of taking care of her grief every day instead of trying to forget it.

Everyone has to find ways to keep their grief moving without getting distracted. The key is to find a healthy way to move with your grief — not away from it, which isn't really possible. Your road map to grieving — all the energy and emotions associated with it, the efforts you make to keep it moving and the advice you receive about it — is inside you. Your grief is a part of you.

When you keep your grief moving, you are helping to level out the grief energy. Have you ever avoided a bad feeling only to explode in angry tears several days later?

Doing things that help us move our grief helps us manage and cope with all the feelings and sensations that come with the grief experience.

Listen, grief can be really intense. The hardest you ever cry in life will probably happen as a part of grief. That is normal. Your instincts are telling you to avoid this intense sadness or anger.

It's important to pay attention to what your grief needs and to recognize that you do have some choices, some control. You get to decide whether to bury or plant it and what activities and tools you will use to move forward with it.

GRiEF IS LiKE A LITTLE KiD, NO MATTER HOW OLD YOU ARE

Grief is like a little kid inside you. A little kid is not old enough to speak well, so they cry or throw tantrums when something is wrong. Grief is like this. If you stop paying attention to that little kid inside you, even just for a day, you can expect a major blowup: "HEY! I NEED ATTENTION!"

This even happens to adults. Many adults are so busy with life — work, family, running errands — that they try to put off what their grief needs. But their grief will overwhelm them eventually and disrupt all that. Think of it like an adult version of a little kid having a meltdown in a grocery store!

Have you ever known a little kid to sit completely still for hours (well, other than in front of a screen)? No, right? That's a lot like our grief. Grief needs to move and grow and change, just like a little kid does. So when we try to ignore our grief, or tell it to just sit quietly and not need anything, it never works. It might work for a little bit, but it never works forever.

TAKE CARE OF YOU

Ask yourself these two questions:

Notice the "today" in both of those questions. Checking in with yourself every day helps you navigate grief energy as it changes. And it can! You might have bursts of needing to move and be loud and connect with others followed by days of needing to lie down quietly and be alone. Some days you might feel like a dog that wants to run for miles, and other days you might feel like a cat that wants to hide under the bed and sleep in a quiet, dark place. You might swing wildly between different energies, and you might be stuck in one gear for a while. It is all normal.

How you keep your grief moving will change as you get older and more experienced with grief, and it will also help you move through your loss more comfortably.

Ultimately, paying attention to your grief energy, and making an effort to keep your grief moving, will help you navigate the weird and wondrous world of grief more smoothly. That out-of-control feeling when you explode with tears you didn't see coming or sweep all of your artwork off your desk to the floor, ruining everything, can make you feel worse. It's easy to become overwhelmed with feelings you don't understand. You need to pay extra-special attention to yourself during this time when it will help the most. Don't put it off ... take care of *you*.

Grievers Share How They Keep Their Grief Moving

This list, submitted by real-life grievers, might inspire you to try new ways of keeping your grief moving.

I like to take my grief to the beach. Letting my feet touch the water and feeling the waves beat against my ankles helps me feel connected to something bigger than myself, which pulls me out of the "sinking inward" feeling I can get when grief hits. Remind my grief that it is only a small part of my life. I will manage it; it will not manage me.   – Candylee W.

I had a mix tape and on one side was all songs that helped me cry. The flip side had the songs that lifted and empowered me. It was a cleansing process for me. Let it out and then lift me up.
– Bonnie Jean F.

Play video games!
– KTZ

Doing nail art! Taking a shower (easy but really helped me!)
– Em M.

Spending time with animals (interacting with pets or watching them in nature). They are so pure and live in the moment.
– Megan H.

Write letters to your lost loved one.
- Sophia E.

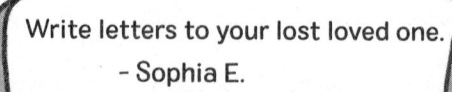

When dealing with the loss of a pet, it helps to face the things they left behind, like a cage or collar, quickly and face the grief. If you avoid it long enough, it ends up bringing back the grief every time. I feel it is easiest to go often to those things and try to think about how many good times you had with them even if it makes you sad. Then it can be a place you go and find happiness and remember their spirit is still with you instead of just making you cry. If you have them in a grave, it is nice to decorate it and make it lovely so you have a place to go to be with them and remember them. You can go often and bring something nice each time, like a flower or pretty rock, so you have a nice area to go when you feel grief again.
– Helena S.

"I feel" statements! They help identify what you are feeling/that your feeling doesn't define you. An example: I feel scared because the world doesn't understand my grief.
- Olivia T.

Try to keep enjoying the activities that you shared with your loved one. It may not look/feel the same but you can enjoy those things in new ways that can help you heal and grow.
- Elle S.

Put on a special song and dance like no one is watching.
- Andrea C.

On my mom's birthday after she passed, I bought a beautiful purple orchid. Orchids were my mom's favorite flower, especially purple ones. So to honor and celebrate my mom on her birthday, I sat out in my garden with the orchid close by, made myself a cup of tea, and talked to her. I know it sounds cliché, but I felt like she was there. Her energy was there, through what that purple orchid meant to me and to my mom, and the good memories started flowing much more than the bad ones. I still felt my grief; it didn't magically disappear, but I understood that my relationship with my mom didn't end when she passed away — it simply evolved. I talk to my purple orchid every other day or so, and it has bloomed and thrived more than any plant I have ever owned.

–Tamar W.

I paint my face with a clay face mask!
- Caitlin B.

Go for a bike ride/skateboard/roller blade or put together/wear an outfit you feel good in.
- Asja B

When I'm grieving I like to remind myself to rest. Taking a nap calms a lot of the anxiety I carry in my body. An hour of rest resets my body and mind and when I wake I find that my grief is much less overwhelming. Checking in with your body's most basic needs is so important when you're grieving.
- Megan W.

Repot, water and rearrange my plants. Tend to all things that are alive.
— Alix R.

Get together with a friend that fills your cup.
— Mitchell M.

Rewatching a movie or show that I've watched a bunch of times.
— Sarah

Sing and/or play a musical instrument! Play your feelings out.
— Jillian R.

Sewing a quilt or creating a collage of tender memories.
— Jenn W.

Collecting and pressing flowers to use in jewelry making.
— Ellie B.

Collect things you find: pennies, dimes, feathers.
— Emily M.

Make a new recipe. Call a friend out of the blue.
— Mary Kate B.

Make photo albums/order prints online. Especially of me and my mom. Rearrange/redecorate my room. Move my favorite trinkets around. Add/remove artwork. Get new flowers/trinkets for Mom's urn. Decorate the shelf I have her on.
    – Ivelisse O.

I allow myself to grieve daily, in ways both large and small.
    – Mika K.

Lego building
    – Veronica R.

I spend time in nature, feeling the earth beneath my feet.
    – Rebekah R.

Carry this with you

1. Grief energy is what the grief experience feels like for you. It can give you clues to help you figure out what you need.

2. Grief is like a seed, and it's up to you to either bury or plant it.

3. Keep your grief moving in whatever way makes sense for you.

WHAT WORKS FOR YOU?

When a deathloss or shadowloss happens, you can feel "stuck" in your grief. That's why it's important to keep your grief moving. Try different ways to keep your grief moving for a week and note how you feel after each "exercise." Remember, any feeling can be a part of grief, so you don't have to wait until you're feeling sad to try an activity. It's important to keep your grief moving through all of the different ways you feel.

Try some ideas shared by real-life grievers on the previous pages or from the list on the next page. Try choosing one activity that you already enjoy doing and, on another day, try one that you wouldn't normally do. How did you feel before each activity? How did you feel after? What else could help you keep your grief moving?

beading

SHOOTING HOOPS

Journaling

Taking a long walk

BAKING

DOODLING

Calling a friend

DECORATING YOUR ROOM

SKATEBOARDING

JAMMING ON A GUITAR

READING A BOOK

SINGING AS LOUD AS YOU CAN

ORGANIZING COLLECTIBLES

Chapter Five

FEELiNGS

How are you feeling right now? When you woke up this morning, and before bed last night, how did you feel then? How would you describe your grief energy? Is your grief making you feel more tired and dull, like there's nothing in the world that you want to do? Or is it making you feel anxious and jittery, like you want to jump out of your own skin?

In that short period of time spent reading the paragraph above, some feelings came and some went, and maybe some stayed the whole time but changed intensity. Our feelings change and shift all the time. We don't always notice them, but they are always there. You don't always notice the tip

of your nose even though you can cross your eyes and look at it right now.

Did you try it?

JACOB

Jacob doesn't love cleaning their room. They'd much rather spend their free time out with friends instead of being stuck inside neatly folding their clothes and cleaning up after the half-dozen art projects they're in the middle of. So any time Jacob has to clean their room, they race to get it over with as fast as possible by stuffing their clothes into whatever drawer in their dresser has the most room, scooping up all their different art projects and piling them on the closet floor, and cramming any leftover things that don't really have a home into the nearest box, tote or desk drawer. Jacob would move in such a frenzy that by the time they were tucking the last few items out of sight under their bed, they wouldn't even really know what the things were that they had just put away. Only later, when Jacob realized that their lucky shirt had gone missing, or they couldn't find a drawing they wanted to finally finish, would it occur to them those things must be buried under a pile of stuff.

Sometimes our feelings seem to disappear or become invisible.

It's probably not surprising that Jacob often loses things or even forgets what they had sitting around in the first place. Out of sight, out of mind, right?

The same thing can happen with our feelings. You may start to feel something that doesn't feel very nice, so you don't want to spend much time with that feeling, the same way Jacob doesn't want to spend much time cleaning their room. So, you decide to stuff that feeling into a back corner of your mind, and you pile a bunch of other things on top of it — all the homework you have to do this week, who you're going to take to the next school dance, what you need to work on to make the softball team.

You might notice you've been angry about something but didn't realize it because it was tucked away. That feeling was there all along; it just might have been out of focus for you because it wasn't fully put away or dealt with.

EMOTIONS VS. FEELINGS

Did you know these are two different words?

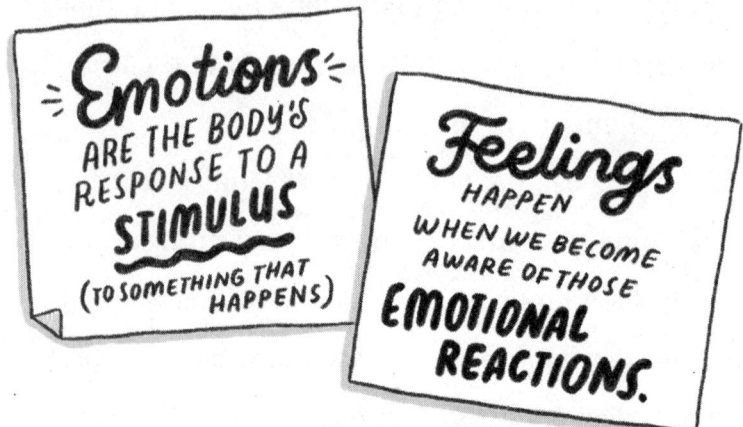

You know how some people's cheeks get bright red when they get embarrassed? That is their body responding to a stimulus. Embarrassment is the feeling that comes after — once you process what those red cheeks mean.

Humans have emotional responses all the time, but we don't have a "feeling" until we become aware of those responses.

An entire science is dedicated to the study of emotions. It's called affective neuroscience. We don't yet fully understand how emotions happen and how feelings emerge, but we do know that emotions and feelings are very, very real. Feelings may just be on the inside, but they have very real effects inside and out. Your feelings give you clues you can use to figure out how to take better care of yourself and what unmet needs you might have. Feelings also tell us when things are going well — when our needs are met. For example, when you are feeling happy, that's probably because in the moment you feel happy, all of your needs are met. When you are feeling angry, that might be because you have an unmet need — you are having to go without something or something was taken from you.

Imagine arriving at school when you suddenly realize that you left your homework on the kitchen counter. It's due today. And you have no way of going home to get it. Your body might physically respond the second you realize you forgot it — your mouth dries out or your muscles tense up. Maybe you clench your jaw. Or your cheeks flash bright red. Those physical responses are part of an emotional response. Those physical signs — the emotional reactions of your body and the emotions shown on your outside — are connected to what you are feeling on the inside. You might feel anxious, distraught, or embarrassed about forgetting your homework.

Most people use the words "feeling" and "emotion" interchangeably. It's helpful to know a little bit about the science behind them both so you can better understand your own body and the unique way you respond to different situations and events.

GRiEF IS A VERB

You'll remember from
Chapter One that it's a
common myth that grief
is a feeling, but it's not. You

can't *feel* grief. You can *grieve* though, which is a verb.
Grieving is an action. It's a process — the process of grief.

You can feel sad. You can feel angry. You can feel happy.
All of those feelings can be a part of the grief response.

Grief includes a mix of feelings that are unique to you and
the loss you are experiencing.

ANY FEELiNG CAN BE A PART OF GRiEF

Did you know that you can experience happiness while
grieving? Also joy. Even relief. These are not inappropriate
feelings, no matter what anyone might say. How can
something you can't control be wrong? It's not wrong to
sneeze if you're allergic to cats. It's not wrong to cough if
water goes up your nose. Those are both ways that your body

automatically reacts to the situation it's in. Feelings are not something you pick and choose — they just happen. Any feeling can be a part of grief!

These are the most common feelings to have when grieving, and you might feel any or many of them:

If you think about a loss you've had, what feelings were a part of your grief response? Have you felt any of the feelings listed above?

Whatever mix of feelings you've had, you are normal. Even if your friends or family have had different feelings than you, that's okay. It's normal to not have the same feelings as everyone around you.

FEELINGS ARE LiKE THE WEATHER

What's the weather like where you are today? Is it hot and sunny? Cold and cloudy? Humid or dry?

What was the weather like yesterday? Basically the same or pretty different?

Like so much of the grief process, feelings are a lot like the weather. You may start the day feeling sunny and bright, but by the afternoon, a thunderstorm rolls in and everything gets darker, colder and wet. Or it might be beautiful most days, but sometimes it's windy or humid rather than a dry heat.

Our feelings can change as often and quickly as weather changes.

What's important to know about all feelings is that they will pass — just like storms, just like clouds.

Sometimes it's easier to ask, "How is your weather today?" instead of asking, "How do you feel?" Relating feelings to the weather makes some people feel less vulnerable. Well-meaning adults might think you shouldn't feel sad or mad. But they can more easily accept hearing that a storm cloud has settled. That language is easier to digest. It also frames feelings as changeable, which they are!

Imagine if everyone showed up at school in the morning and your teacher asked, "How is everyone's weather today?" Not everyone will have the same answers, but it suddenly becomes a lot easier to understand not only how you are feeling but what everyone else might be feeling, too. If it's raining for Bao, she might need a little extra kindness today. And if you are feeling sunny, maybe you can share some of that with others.

This simple exercise can really help families, especially if the whole family is grieving. Because it's normal for everyone to have good days and bad days, it can really help to know who might need to borrow an umbrella.

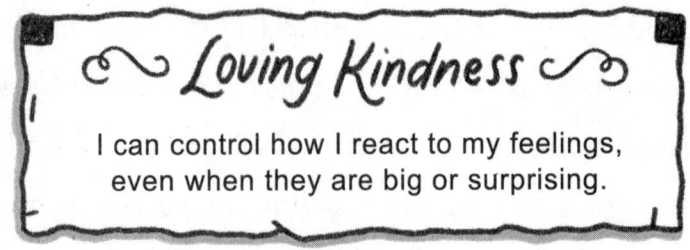

STORMS EVENTUALLY GO AWAY

What do you do when you are having a really strong feeling?

Or, put another way, what do you do when there's a really bad storm?

When you have a really powerful sad feeling, you might be scared of how deeply you are feeling it. You might even think, "I have never been this sad in my entire life." In times like that, you want to make sure you are keeping yourself safe and protected to get through that storm. On those bad days, you could say to a friend or trusted adult, "My weather is really rough today." Then you can take the time you need to figure out how to get through that storm. Maybe on those bad days you need a comfy blanket, your favorite movie on the TV and your favorite snacks. Maybe you need friends to text you their favorite memories from last summer. A cozy environment and connection with others can help make the thunderstorms of life less scary.

WHAT HAPPENS WHEN WE IGNORE OUR FEELINGS?

There are going to be some days when you have so much going on that you don't have time to feel your feelings! And on other days, you will be so sick of feeling them that you will just want a break.

The grieving process can be annoying. There will be days when you wish you could take a sick day from grief. There might even be days when you yell,

CAN I JUST GET OVER IT TODAY?!

It's normal to have days like that. On those days, give yourself a break from grief. Remember Emma? When they were first grieving, they scrolled social media to ignore and avoid uncomfortable feelings. After they learned healthy ways to keep their grief moving and better ways to feel their feelings, they got to a point where they knew when it was okay to tune grief out for a little while. Sometimes, in your grief journey, you might have a day where you are just tired of grieving.

Tired of checking in with yourself, talking about your weather and feeling your feelings. Tired of dealing with it. It's okay sometimes to give yourself an afternoon to just zone out on social media.

But what happens when we try to "turn off" or "ignore" our feelings for more than a day or two? When we suppress (to hide or to minimize) feelings for too long, some pretty serious things can happen.

Our feelings let us know about the state of our bodies and minds. They let us know when there might be problems. Our feelings let us know what we might need, so ignoring them means ignoring our needs — ignoring ourselves.

Have you ever left a plate or a bowl with a little food on it somewhere in your room? You ignore it and tell yourself you'll take it to the kitchen later. Well, after a few days, that little bit of food has turned into something that smells bad and is growing mold. It's now a bigger mess to clean up than if you had just dealt with it on the first day. Oops!

When something serious like a shadowloss or a deathloss happens, your brain might try to help you by distracting you from your feelings. *I'll deal with it later*, you might think. Your brain might be trying to protect you from the loss. Feeling our feelings means we have accepted that the deathloss or shadowloss happened. If we don't feel those feelings, then we don't have to face how much that loss has truly affected us.

The grief response affects us behaviorally, cognitively, emotionally, physically, spiritually and socially. Who wouldn't want to skip all that?!

You might try to suppress or ignore your feelings because that's what you were taught to do. You might have a parent who never shows or shares emotions or who taught you that feelings should be hidden. If you grew up with these ideas, how would you know how to act differently?

Boys, in particular, are often taught that they should not be emotional. They might be told to be strong and that emotions are a sign of weakness. But all people have feelings. Your gender or sex has nothing to do with it.

Suppressing or ignoring our feelings for a long time has very serious impacts on our physical and mental health, including raising blood pressure, reducing self-esteem and worsening memory. Suppressing emotions for a long time can literally make you sick.

Loving Kindness

I accept all of my feelings.

LET IT OUT

It can be really scary or uncomfortable to share our feelings with others. It's okay to share your feelings with some people in your life and not with others. What's important is that you are close enough to at least one adult you can talk to about these things. That might be a parent, religious leader, older relative, teacher or counselor. That adult will have had more practice with shadowlosses, deathlosses, grief. It is one thing to tell yourself that this storm will pass; it's a whole other thing to hear someone talk about their storms and for you to see them embody moving forward through grief. That can be powerfully reassuring. You can also talk to your friends, too, of course. We'll talk more about this in Chapter Eight.

Maybe you want a break from grieving and you don't feel like sharing your feelings. It's okay to say — even to a well-meaning adult — "Thank you for asking, but I don't want to talk right now. Can we talk about this later?"

There are a couple exceptions here. If you are thinking about hurting yourself or are having such strong feelings

JACOB

When Jacob was little, they and their cousin were outside on the grass surrounded by a dozen toys. The sun was shining and the sky was bright blue. Jacob's little cousin was feeling cranky that day, despite the perfect weather, and wanted every single toy Jacob touched. Jacob was incredibly patient with their cousin. For more than an hour, all Jacob did was pick up a toy and hand it over to their little cousin one after the other. Jacob was happy to do what they could to make others happy, and to this day they're still like that.

For Jacob's most recent birthday, Jacob's mom gifted them a beautiful red leather journal with gold edges. She said, "You are always worried about others, Jacob. You need to make some time for yourself, too." Jacob began to write their thoughts and feelings in this journal. It became a safe place to express how they really felt about things happening in their life, like when they were upset to hear their parents arguing.

Jacob realized that they were much more comfortable listening to and supporting others as they dealt with challenges rather than being the one to share. They preferred to keep their feelings in their journal.

As Jacob wrote more and more in their journal, they got better at noticing their own feelings and discovered new feelings they didn't even know they had before.

that you are scared or are putting other people or animals in harm's way, you need to tell an adult. Sharing what's going on with an adult can get you additional help, tools and resources that in turn can help you feel better.

CALL OR TEXT 988
IF YOU NEED SOMEONE
TO TALK TO AND ARE IN
THE UNITED STATES
OR CANADA.
THERE IS SOMEONE
THERE FOR YOU 24/7.

There might also be times when someone you care about is grieving and they don't feel like sharing their feelings with you. When people let you know they aren't ready to talk about something, it's not because you aren't a good or trustworthy person; it just means that they simply aren't ready to talk about it. Just as everyone grieves in a unique way, everyone has a different level of comfort with talking about their feelings or about the details of a deathloss or shadowloss. If your friend isn't ready to talk, you could offer an alternative. Perhaps you could watch a movie together, kick around a ball or listen to music. Sometimes just being there can be more helpful and supportive.

Feelings and whether we are ready to share them or not can be complicated because there is no specific timeline for when or how that should happen. Be patient with your friends and yourself, and know that anytime someone asks how you are feeling, it's because they care about you. Just like we all have a different mix of feelings while grieving, we have different ways of sharing those feelings with others.

ANiMALS ... THEY'RE JUST LiKE US! OR ARE WE JUST LiKE THEM?

Just as people experience feelings, so too do many animals. And just as we experience grief, the same is true for many kinds of animals.

Many scientists are studying the emotional experiences of animals. For example, we now know that chickens experience both positive and negative emotions, and some research shows they also experience empathy. We also know that chickens have unique personalities, just like people.

Grief affects the animal kingdom as well. Elephants will gather around the dead body of their loved one, smelling and touching them, and returning for visits. When another dog in their home dies, dogs will become lethargic (lying around, not wanting to play), may not eat and seem sad. And when a mother dolphin's baby dies, she will often carry the body around the ocean for many days. Just as loss is hard for people to deal with, it's also hard for many animals, too.

And let's not forget how comforting a snuggle with your dog can be after a hard day. Our pets seem to be able to detect when we're feeling down. Have you ever had a pet drop a toy in your lap as if to say, "Here's my favorite toy to make you feel better"?

Pets are also great listeners, and they will never tell you to stop crying. When dealing with loss, it can help to talk things out with your cat first before sharing what you're thinking and feeling with an adult. Animals can give us a nonjudgmental space to process big experiences because they love us unconditionally and don't have expectations of us. You never have to worry about snot dripping out of your nose with the family dog because he probably licks his own butt, right?

∽ Loving Kindness ∽

I have not been buried in grief; I have been planted with grief. It takes time to bloom.

Carry this with you

1. Emotions are a physical response to something, and feelings are what you feel about it.

2. Any feeling can be a part of your grief experience.

3. It's not healthy to avoid our feelings for very long.

WHAT EMOTIONS LOOK LiKE FOR YOU

Emotions show up physically in our bodies in different ways for each of us. We can get stronger at managing our unique feelings just by paying attention to how they show up. Take a look at these Feelings Bracelets flowcharts and choose one physical sensation you notice in your body today. Let's say you pick "tight jaw." If you move through the flowchart from the "tight jaw" sensation, you'll see that it is closely linked to "irritated," and if you move further down that it is closely linked to "anger." Decide for yourself if your "tight jaw" sensation might be connected to some anger you are feeling in life right now. Just being aware of your sensations and the feelings they can be connected to can sometimes bring us a little more peace. Feelings are like friendship bracelets — they remind you of yourself and what's important in life.

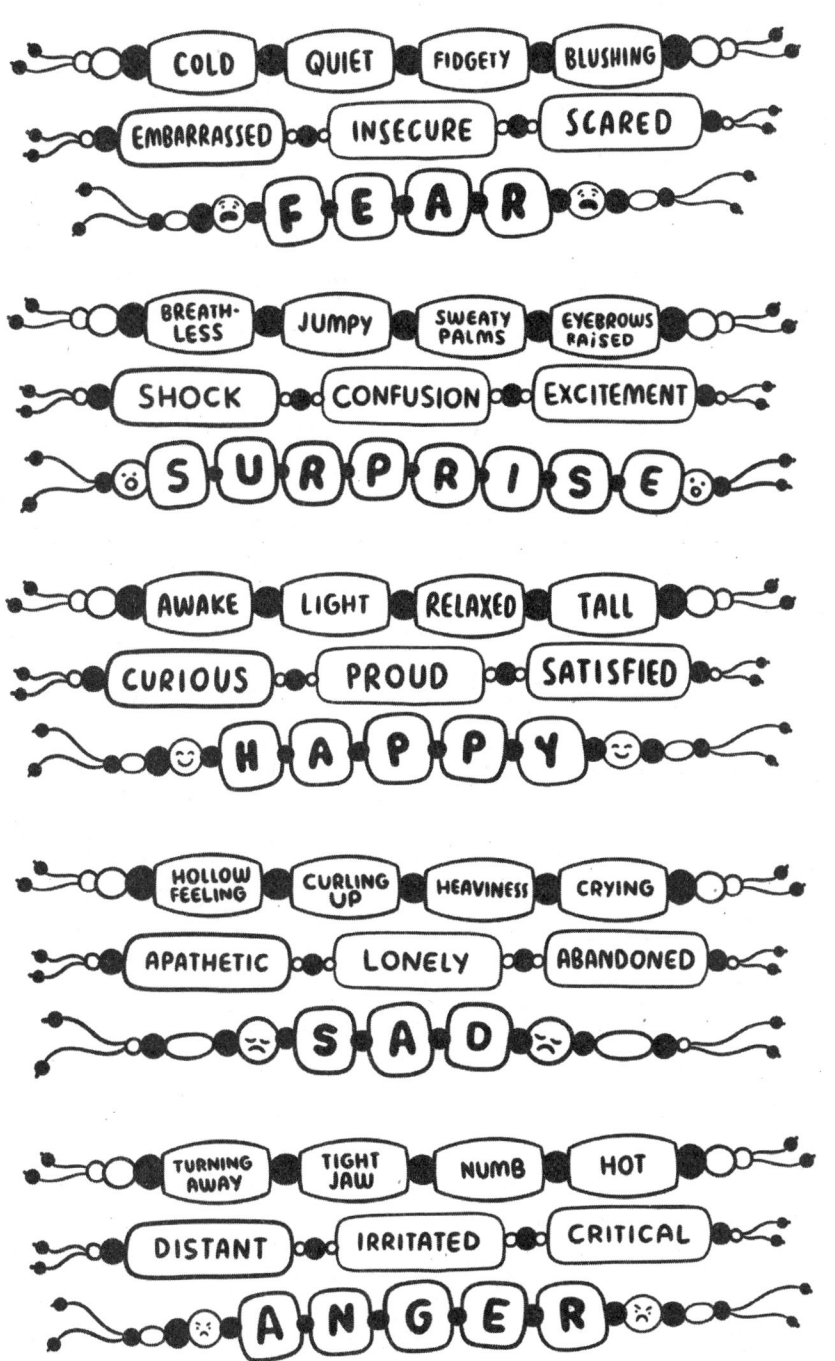

Chapter Six

MEANiNGFUL HEALiNG

When we go through setbacks or disappointments, life can feel different for a little while but eventually it goes "back to normal." You cannot go "back to normal" after a deathloss or a shadowloss because what you lost is no longer there to go back to.

We heal from grief but don't really recover. You will always be moving with your grief. It won't always be so intense, and many days of your life you won't even notice it. It's something we learn to live with; it's something we learn to carry with us as we grow up.

If you break your leg, when the cast comes off after a few weeks, the doctor might say, "Your bones are all healed. You're as good as new!" At no point, after a deathloss or a shadowloss, would a doctor ever say, "Okay, you are completely done grieving and good as new!"

HEAL WiTH MEANiNG

Grief is not a virus or sickness. Grief is also not an injury like appendicitis, a concussion or a broken wrist. These are all things that happen to your body, that your physical body will try to fight off, heal from or heal around. There

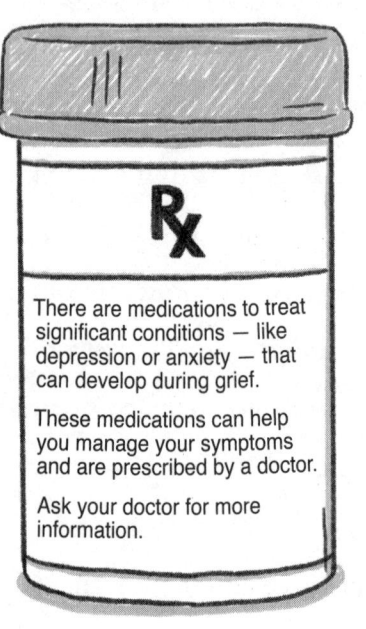

There are medications to treat significant conditions — like depression or anxiety — that can develop during grief.

These medications can help you manage your symptoms and are prescribed by a doctor.

Ask your doctor for more information.

are also medicines for most of these things. You might take an antibiotic if you have bronchitis. Or pain medicine if you break your wrist.

There is no pill to treat grief, no grief syrup to ease your pain.

Yet grief affects us as much as an illness or injury can. There are signs of grief just like there are symptoms of a cold. A picture of you while you are grieving might show evidence of that grief on your face. A trash can full of tear-soaked tissues in your bedroom also shows your grief. Grief leaves proof that it's there, scattered throughout different parts of your life.

But while your heart or your spirits or even your brain might feel broken, grief is not something to fix. You are grieving because everything once made sense and now it doesn't. You loved and still love what you lost, whether it's a shadowloss or a deathloss, and missing and mourning that is the right and normal experience.

Every time you grieve, you will discover new things about your grief and about what you are grieving that are special to you. These special things have meaning only to you and will help you heal. This is meaningful healing.

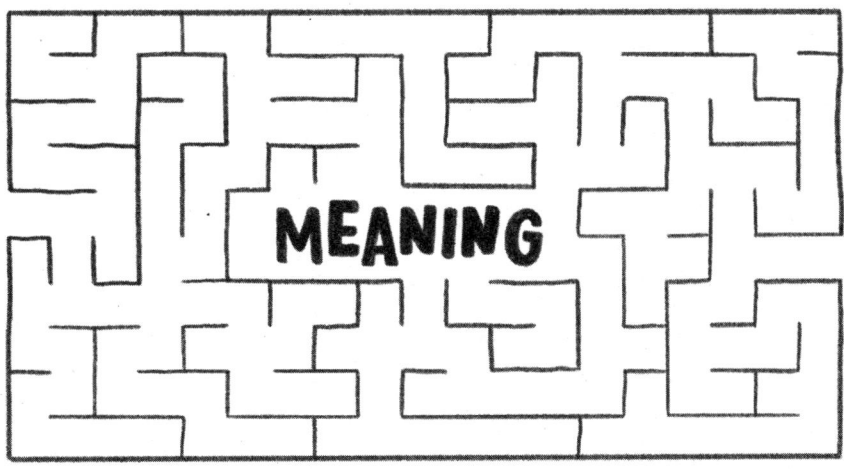

Finding meaning in healing is actually a really important factor in whether or not people heal in a healthy way from a loss. Finding meaning will help you become more resilient. Resilience is our ability to get back up after we are knocked down, and meaning is about finding your reason for even wanting to get back up again.

Meaning can come from anything and everything. It can be taking a walk in a special place, eating a certain kind of food, wearing a certain kind of outfit, picking a certain color flower or watching a favorite movie every year over winter break. Or it can just be a regular part of your routine that makes you feel good. It doesn't have to be grand or magnificent to have meaning. Often enough, the things that are most meaningful in life are ordinary things. It's very important to think about and find the things that are meaningful to you in your grief process. Those meaningful things can become sources of resilience, kind of like extra energy boosters that help us want to get back up after we fall down. Instead of falling flat on the ground, things that are sources of meaning for you can make it seem like you've only fallen on a trampoline instead.

HOW TO FiND MEANiNG iN YOUR LOSS

For a deathloss, think about the person or animal you lost
and what you will miss about them. For a shadowloss, think
about what you lost and what you will miss about it. How
can you honor that in your life now, even though it is gone
or different? Maybe your shadowloss is moving, because you
lost touch with your neighborhood friends, changed schools
and miss your old house. Or, maybe your shadowloss is your
parents' divorce. It could be the COVID-19 pandemic and
everything it took from you: sports to in-person parties to
in-person school.

Finding meaning takes time. It can take weeks and even
years after a loss to find meaning. It's possible to keep
finding meaningful things throughout your whole life.

So if it's still early in your grief process, give yourself time.

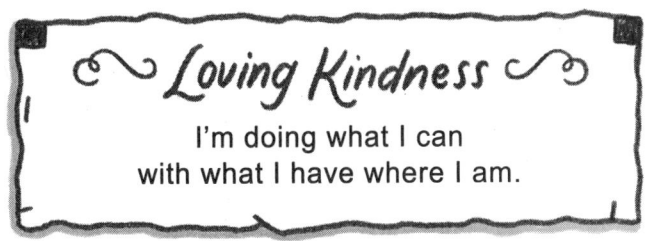

Loving Kindness
I'm doing what I can
with what I have where I am.

THiS SOUP CALLED LiFE

If a chef poured some plain
water in a pot, heated it up
and called it soup, you
wouldn't consider it soup,
right? It's just water. No
flavor. There's nothing in it!

What if she added some
onion, celery, garlic and a
little salt and pepper? That
might technically be soup,
but is it a soup you'd enjoy? It
definitely wouldn't fill you up!

How about if she added some chicken, matzah balls,
carrots and fresh herbs? Maybe a squeeze of tomato paste
and a little bit of anchovy to add flavor. Now that's some
soup! Matzah ball soup! You'd probably want a bowl of that
and might even ask for the recipe.

As you move through life, you collect new experiences.
Think of those experiences as ingredients — ingredients in
your unique soup of life.

We collect rewarding experiences during our whole life.
Making a new friend. Starting another grade in school.

Going on a field trip or vacation. Learning to play an instrument.

We also collect challenging experiences like struggling at math, dealing with bullying or saying goodbye to a loved one who died.

A good soup has all kinds of ingredients. On their own, each ingredient might taste okay, and some might even taste bad.

Have you ever tasted tomato paste straight out of the metal tube or can? Or an anchovy by itself? That flavor is overwhelming to most people.

But if you mix a little bit of that anchovy in with everything else in the soup, it makes the whole thing taste better. The flavor becomes more complex and deeper. It turns a good soup into a great soup. It's amazing how adding a pungent, salty fish to a pot of water and vegetables makes it all taste better.

When we deal with a really challenging experience, or even a negative one, at some point we discover how the worst moments of our lives actually made us better in some ways.

Loving Kindness

I can try new things and face challenges.

That doesn't mean a bad experience is less bad or that you should be glad it happened. It just means that as time goes by, we can start to see how that bad experience taught us some positive lessons or made us better people. We learn from both challenging experiences *and* rewarding ones.

By the time you are old, you want your life to be an amazing soup full of all kinds of interesting ingredients. You want your life soup to be so interesting that people want the recipe. You want them to take one taste and exclaim, "Oh my gosh, what is that ingredient I'm tasting? I've never had anything like this before!" You want to be proud of your soup and all the amazing ingredients you learned about and have collected throughout your life.

Loving Kindness
The bad days help me
appreciate the good days.

In life, we cannot make a great soup from only sweet ingredients. Sometimes we need the salty, the spicy and the bitter, too. A well-lived life means you've had good days and bad days, and they're all important in helping you become who you uniquely are.

WHAT GOOD CAN POSSIBLY COME FROM GRIEF?

Did you know that there are three very special skills that people get better at because of grief? After a loss, many people become more resilient, empathetic and present.

Remember, resilience is your ability to get back up after you fall down.

But that means you have to fall down in the first place. You become more resilient through practice. You don't become more resilient by doing nothing. Challenges have to happen in your life in order for your resilience to grow.

Empathy is the second skill humans develop through facing challenges. Empathy is the ability to understand and share the feelings of another person.

A good way to understand empathy is by comparing it to sympathy. Sympathy means understanding a situation from your own perspective while empathy means understanding it from another's perspective. Sympathy is "at you" while empathy is "with you." Sympathy and empathy are both helpful because they help us relate to and connect with others in different ways.

Presence means being able to be in the here and now — to be in the moment. In this very moment. We'll talk more about presence in Chapter Eight.

WHAT iS RESILIENCE?

When people say you're resilient, that's a compliment. It means you are good at bouncing back or trying again. It means you are strong. Have you ever heard the saying "Get back in the saddle" or "Get back on the horse"? That means that after a failure, setback or loss, you get right back up again in the saddle of life.

When a deathloss or shadowloss happens, those losses can really put life on hold. That's normal and totally okay. These experiences can help us learn how to "get back in the saddle" of life when we are ready again. We are ready when we have felt all of our feelings, kept our grief moving, read all the signs and see that a new normal has started to take shape. These experiences help us become more resilient.

Why is it good to be resilient? If you are resilient, you are good at adapting to challenges, dealing with difficulty and coping with tough stuff in healthy ways.

WHAT iS EMPATHY?

Empathy means that you can understand and share in the feelings of another person.

For example, let's say you move away and have to go to a new school. When you get to the new school, you find out that one of your classmates also moved away and this is a new school for them, too. You can empathize with that classmate because you know what it's like to move and be the new kid at school.

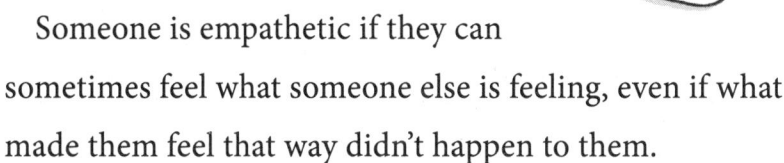

Someone is empathetic if they can sometimes feel what someone else is feeling, even if what made them feel that way didn't happen to them.

Have you ever seen a little kid fall down and start crying and then the little kid's best friend starts crying, too, even though they didn't fall? That's empathy.

Shadowlosses and deathlosses help us to become more empathetic.

This might be tough: think of a deathloss or a shadowloss you've experienced.

Now imagine that you make a new friend, and you find out that they had a similar kind of deathloss or shadowloss that you did. The tough feelings now have an outlet. You know you have a safe and understanding space to share your feelings if you want to. While your grief experiences would still be different, you can empathize with each other because you both will know what it's like to have gone through the same kind of thing.

Why is it good to be empathetic? It means you are sensitive to and aware of other people's feelings and needs. People who are empathetic tend to be better at forming and keeping relationships. Research tells us that people who are good at connecting with others have better physical and mental health.

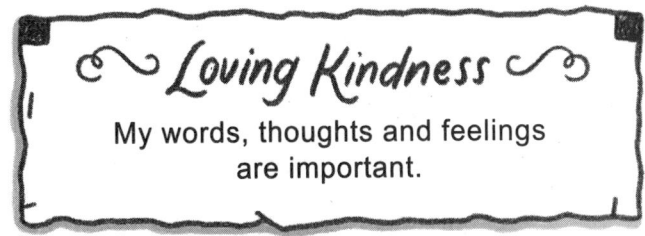

THE SPECIAL INGREDIENT IS GRIEF

Grief is challenging. Grief will change you. Grief is definitely a bitter ingredient on its own, but, like anchovies, if you add it to your life soup, the flavor becomes deeper and richer. When people want to know what that special something is, you get to tell them the wonderful stories of how you got those ingredients — the good and the bad — and you can find healing, resilience and empathy, for yourself and others.

Carry this with you

1. Grief is not something to fix because nothing has been broken. Grief is something you experience.

2. Meaning can be found in anything. It's important to have things in your life that are meaningful to you.

3. Grief can help us become more resilient, empathetic and present.

BEAMING LOVE INTO YOURSELF

Find a comfortable spot to sit or lie flat on your back. It can be on your bed, in a chair, against a tree or somewhere you feel most comfortable. Close your eyes and place one hand over your heart and the other hand over your belly button. With your eyes still closed, imagine the outline of a heart shape surrounding you. What color is the heart shape? How big is it? Notice what your heart shape looks like.

When you inhale, imagine a ball of light tracing around the heart shape, kind of like how a sparkler burns bright or how a lighting bug flashes. As you inhale, push your belly all the way out. Keep your hand over your belly button to feel it fully expand with air. One inhale should equal that little ball of light tracing around the entire heart shape. When you exhale, imagine the ball of light chasing the outline of the heart shape again and feel your belly release the air. Repeat and do this eight times.

As you sit there imagining the heart shape surrounding you, with one hand on your belly and the other over your heart, try saying to yourself, "I am loved. I love myself. I am safe. I will get through this. I am okay." You may have other words that come to mind, and that's okay, too, as long as they are loving words.

When we are grieving, it can feel really nice to beam a little love into ourselves from ourselves.

I AM LOVED
I LOVE MYSELF
I AM SAFE
I WILL GET
THROUGH THIS
I AM OKAY

Chapter Seven

RELIGION, CULTURE AND FAMILIES

Another way to think about grief is like this — ⌠outside grief⌡ and ⌠inside grief⌡. Outside grief is all the ways we show and express our grief to others, and inside grief is all the ways we show and express that grief to just ourselves.

Outside grief is often guided by our religion, our culture, our families or a combination of those.

Inside grief is guided by our own independent hearts and minds. It's uniquely, privately yours (unless you decide to share it). No one gets to know your thoughts, feelings and experiences unless you choose to share them.

In your grief journey, you might discover some of the different ways other cultures and communities handle loss. In the process, you might learn that you find comfort in ideas about death and loss from those different perspectives.

Dealing with loss is universal — every culture, every community, every family and every person has to deal with it at some point. Learning how cultures, communities and families outside your own navigate the world of grief can deepen your experience with your own losses and help you learn about the whole world in a new way.

OUTSiDE GRiEF AND RELiGiON

Did you know that most religions have special events, rituals and prayers that recognize death and dying? Funerals, visitations, wakes and special services are some of these religious traditions.

There are often special tools and rituals for people who are grieving as well.

In the Jewish faith, people who are grieving a loved one say a special prayer called *Kaddish* for a certain amount of time after the death. For most mourners, Kaddish is said for 30 days. For children grieving the loss of a parent, Kaddish is said for 11 or 12 months. And every single year on the anniversary of the person's death (called a *yahrzeit*) a candle or special light is lit.

In Buddhism, a special service happens 100 days after a funeral. The grievers acknowledge that the soul of their loved one has moved on.

In Hinduism, one year after the loved one's death, the family will hold a special memorial service called a *shraddha*. During this special ritual, prayers are said, food is eaten and gifts are offered.

There are many religious traditions around the globe that relate to death and grief. It's also important to know that these traditions can vary from place to place. For example, what's normal for a Jewish family in Los Angeles, California, might be a little different than what's normal for a Jewish family in London, England.

Grief, Culture and Family Traditions

Your idea of what is normal when it comes to death, dying, grief and shadowloss most likely comes from your family. We learn what to do and how to act from our families and all the other people we grew up around.

Because we are surrounded by people who do and say the same things when there is a loss, it can be easy to forget that what is normal for you and your community might seem completely bizarre to someone else!

Sometimes you might feel totally out of place in your community (your family, neighborhood or religious community) if the way you want to express your outside grief differs from what your community says is okay to do.

For example, you might not want to show any emotion publicly as you grieve, but maybe your whole family is very comfortable openly crying together. Or, it might be the opposite — you might wish you could openly cry together, but it's not normal or accepted to do that in your family group.

If your outside grief clashes with the way things are "usually done," it doesn't mean something is wrong with you or that you are not being a good family member or member of your religious community. It just means that your grief might have different needs.

This is why it's important to pay attention to both your inside grief and your outside grief.

Loving Kindness

Lots of people love and care about me.

OUTSIDE GRIEF VS. INSIDE GRIEF

Just like we check in with the weather of our grief, it can be helpful to ask ourselves what our outside grief needs versus our inside grief. Does one need more attention?

Being able to notice these things — when our outside grief feels bad and our inside grief feels good, for example — helps us take better care of ourselves. Sometimes there's not much we can do to change things quickly, but just being able to notice it — that helps.

Inside grief activities:

Taking eight slow, deep breaths

Writing a story inspired by the shadowloss or deathloss

Remembering

Putting a picture or object in a special spot in your room that reminds you of the deathloss or shadowloss

Putting on music that you associate with your loss

Meditating

Drawing your feelings

Writing a poem about your loss

Praying

Journaling

Outside grief activities:

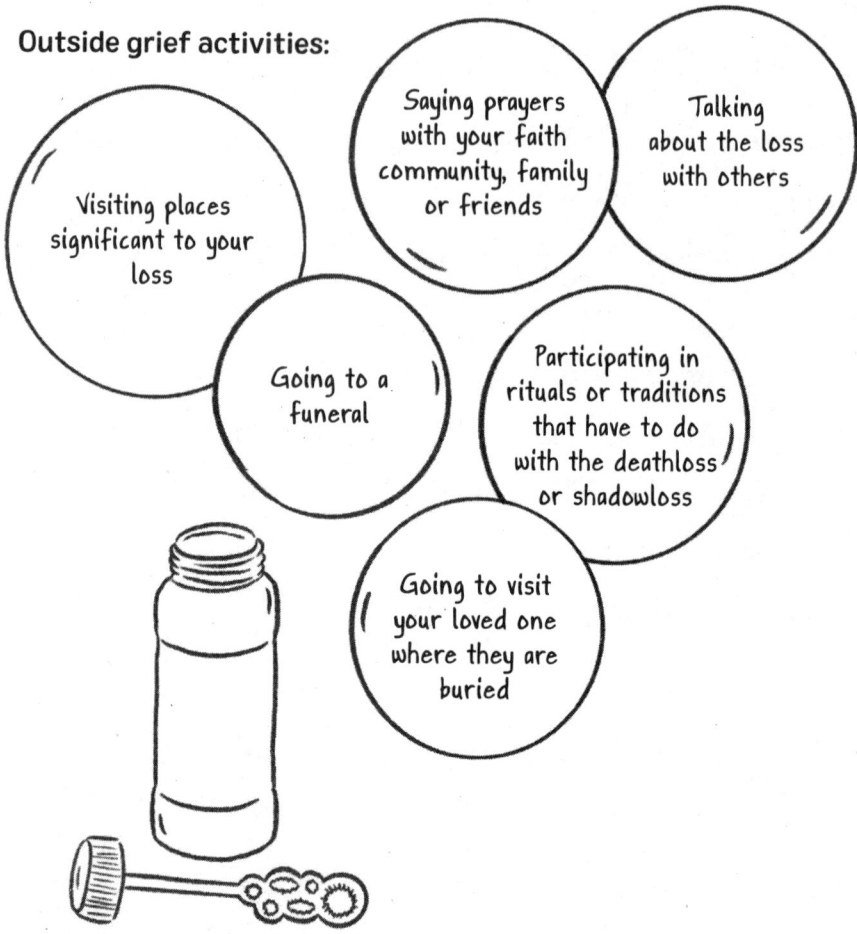

Visiting places significant to your loss

Saying prayers with your faith community, family or friends

Talking about the loss with others

Going to a funeral

Participating in rituals or traditions that have to do with the deathloss or shadowloss

Going to visit your loved one where they are buried

The point of thinking about grief this way is to give you a different way of connecting with it. When you have different ways of thinking about your grief experience, you are more likely to find different ways of handling it.

Ultimately, your grief experience is unique. What works for you might not work for others. You will try things that bring a sense of peace and calmness, and you'll also try things that, well, don't.

As you move through the grieving process alongside your family or friends, you will probably notice differences in outside grief activities most of all. You might see a family member leave church and feel *so much* better. Maybe you feel a little better after going to church, too, but not as much as they do. That's normal, and it's part of learning about how unique the grief experience can really be.

Loving Kindness

Just because I haven't done it before,
doesn't mean I can't.

Carry this with you

1. Outside grief is the way we show and express our grief to others, and inside grief is the way we show and express that grief to just ourselves.

2. Your grief is unique.

3. If the way your outside grief looks is different from others, that doesn't mean anything is wrong with you.

YOUR COMMUNITY OF CARE

On this page you'll see outlines of people and animals all forming the shape of a heart. Everyone has a group of people and animals who care about them. It can be really amazing to see all the people who care about you when you take the time to write out their names. This page can remind you about the caring community of people surrounding you.

Get your journal or a piece of paper and sketch outlines of the people and animals who love you. (Or if it's easier, just doodle a bunch of hearts!). Write the name of a person or animal who cares about you into each outline. You should include family members, friends, classmates, neighbors, teachers, counselors, coaches, doctors, dentists, librarians, bus drivers, people from your religious community if you have one, and pets. What other people can you add?

Chapter Eight

WHEN A FRIEND GRIEVES

There are three ways we talk about time — the past, the present and the future.

One way we spend time in the past is by ⌐ruminating⌐. We ruminate when we rehash events of the past over and over in our mind.

One way we spend time in the future is called ⌐worry⌐. We worry when we think of things that could happen or might happen. Sometimes we worry about things that are very, very unlikely to happen. There is a difference between preparation (thinking about things that will likely happen and working backward from that to make sure you are ready) and worry (thinking about things.that

are unlikely to happen and feeling like there's not much you can do to be ready).

Whether you are ruminating or worrying, you aren't in the here and now. You aren't in the present.

DIYA

It had been a couple of weeks since Diya's classmate had died. She was thinking about a birthday party. She sat on an old rubber tire hanging from a tree in her front yard, but she wasn't swinging. If you looked at her cell phone in her pocket, you'd see eleven unread text messages. If you opened her email, you'd see five opened emails, none of them answered. Diya had been invited to a friend's birthday party last weekend and then didn't show up. When she was invited, she'd said yes right away, but she didn't tell her brother, who normally dropped her off and picked her up from things. The party came and went, and Diya just ... did nothing. Now she was avoiding her friends at school — not sitting with them at lunch but also avoiding them in the hallways between classes. Everything was just such a mess now — she couldn't do anything right — and Diya didn't know how to fix it.

You probably understand that the way Diya has been acting isn't because she's mean; it's because she's grieving. Being overwhelmed can be a part of anyone's grief experience and it can be hard to know what to do to help a friend you think might be experiencing this.

Have you ever tried to talk to someone while they were looking at their phone? They were not fully present for you, and they were not fully present in the moment. They were staying connected to things outside of the here and now.

Learning to be present is a skill that can really help us be there for our friends who are grieving and also for ourselves.

HOW PRESENCE HELPS US SUPPORT OTHERS

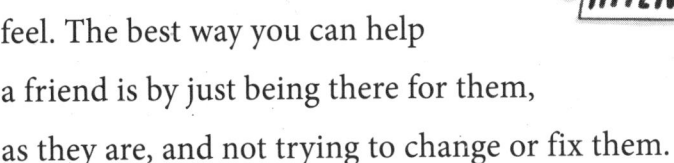

If your friend is grieving, you are not responsible for changing the way that they feel. The best way you can help a friend is by just being there for them, as they are, and not trying to change or fix them.

Have you told a friend a story, and as you spoke, maybe they gasped or exclaimed, "No way!" at dramatic parts or their brow furrowed at sad or strange parts? Making eye contact and reacting is part of being present, but there's more to it. Someone who is present not only gives you their full attention, but they also don't try to tell you how you could have done something better or tell you what you did wrong. They just listened. They heard you. They asked you questions about your experience. They weren't judgmental. That is being present.

And what is a present? A present is a gift. It is a wonderful feeling to have a friend who just wants to hear the good, the bad and the ugly from you but doesn't want to change you or try to take your problems on as projects.

To be present for a grieving friend, you could say something like, "You are my friend and I want to keep being your friend. I think you might be overwhelmed, and I wanted to know if I could help. How can I help you right now?"

Your friend might decline your help, and that's okay. It's enough to reassure them that you are still friends and that you want to keep being friends.

Being there for a friend means that you want to know how they're doing, what they're feeling, what's been going well and what's been going poorly. It means you are willing to roll up your sleeves and help.

Loving Kindness

I am a good friend.

SUPPORTIVE QUESTIONS

The way you ask questions can make a big difference.
For example, imagine being asked one of the following
two questions:

The first question probably feels a little accusatory; it
sounds like something *is* wrong with you, like you are
somehow a problem. The second question is asked without
any accusation — it's asked with invitation. It is asked with
curiosity. Instead of asking, "What can I do?" try asking,
"How can I be there for you right now?" or, "How can I
support you?"

Sometimes it can be a burden for someone who is
grieving to think of ways people can help them. It adds to
their mental load. Tackling an everyday task for them can
be a surprisingly impactful way to help. This can include
dropping library books off, picking up snacks or doing one
of their chores, like mowing the lawn.

Do This Not That

How to Help a Grieving Friend

While there is no one perfect way to respond or to support someone you care about, here are some good ground rules.

DON'T	DO
Don't compare grief No one else has experienced their grief.	**Ask questions** You can connect by showing curiosity about their experience.
Don't fact-check or correct Especially in early grief, facts and timelines can be confused.	**Respect their experience** It's not important who's "more" correct.
Don't minimize Even if you might think their grief is out of proportion to their situation.	**Remember this grief is theirs** Grief belongs to the griever. Your opinions are irrelevant.
Don't give compliments When someone is in pain, they don't need to be reminded how wonderful they are.	**Trust your friend** All the things you love about the person will help them through this experience.
Don't be a cheerleader When things are dark, it's okay to be dark.	**Mirror their reality** When they say, "This sucks," say, "Yes, it does."
Don't talk about "later" Right now, in this present moment, that future is irrelevant.	**Stay in the present moment** Or if the person is talking about the past, join them.
Don't evangelize When something has worked for you, it's tempting to prescribe it for others.	**Trust their self-care** They know themselves best. What works for you may not be for them.
Don't start with solutions In most cases, people need to feel heard, not to be "fixed."	**Get consent** Ask before you offer advice or strategies.

Printed with permission from Megan Devine of Refuge in Grief. Please contact refugeingrief.com for permission to use or reprint.

Above all, show your love.
Be willing to stand beside the gaping hole that has opened in your friend's life, without flinching or turning away. Your steadiness of presence is the absolute best thing you can give.

It's also good to tell your friend you care about them and they're important to you.

Truly supporting a friend means that you choose to walk alongside them in their experience. You are not there to judge, correct or change them.

You are there for them to lean on if they need it and there to cheer them on the whole way. Being present means keeping your friend company as they move through the events of their life.

TOXIC POSITIVITY

Some people are so uncomfortable with grief they might respond to someone's difficult experience or emotions by saying something kind of thoughtless:

Toxic positivity occurs when someone avoids or ignores the negative experience someone is having by using overly positive language. Most people do this because they don't know what else to say to someone who is grieving. But these messages to "be positive" are toxic because they ignore the reality of grief and its very real, challenging feelings.

It is important to acknowledge whatever feelings your grieving friends have. You can say, "It makes sense that you would be sad" and, "This is so hard," but resist the urge to tell them to think of something positive about what has happened. We know that grief is not something that can be fixed!

BEING SEEN

You've learned about presence and toxic positivity in this chapter, which can help you better understand how to support other people as they grieve. There is a third piece to this puzzle: affirmation.

To affirm means "to acknowledge or agree with." It means to say "yes" to something. Affirmation is a positive thing, but it's not toxic positivity.

When you are trying to support a friend, affirmation is something helpful you can give to that person.

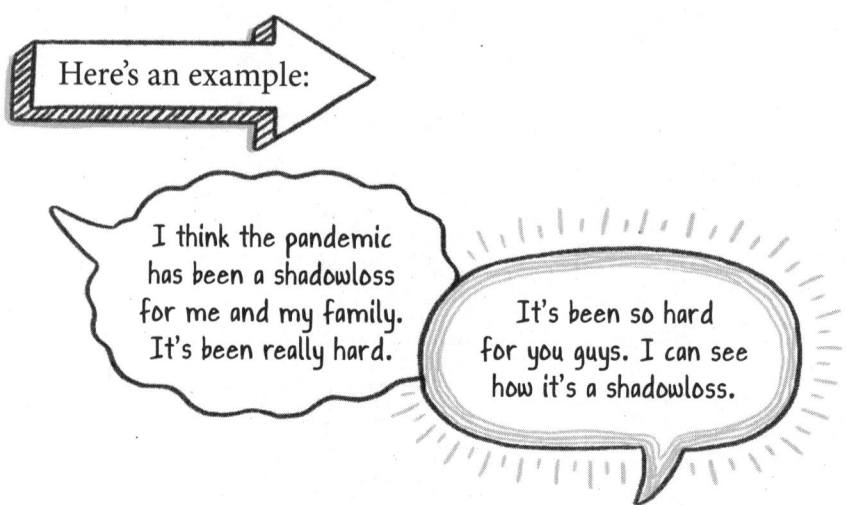

Here's an example:

I think the pandemic has been a shadowloss for me and my family. It's been really hard.

It's been so hard for you guys. I can see how it's a shadowloss.

You aren't trying to offer solutions or telling them to "think positive" (which would be toxic positivity); you are acknowledging what they are saying and affirming their experience.

Sometimes shadowlosses and deathlosses make us feel awful. Good friends by our side affirming our experience and not judging us for it, or trying to fix it for us, can make us feel a little less awful.

Shadowlosses and deathlosses are a normal part of life. Knowing about how to support others through their grief means that we can get better at asking for what we need, too.

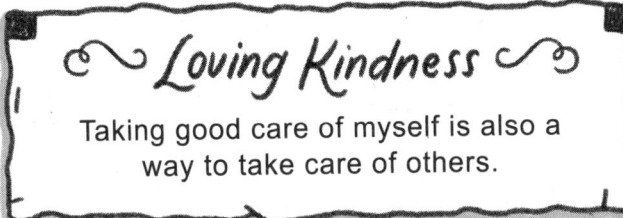

∞ *Loving Kindness* ∞

Taking good care of myself is also a way to take care of others.

Carry this with you

1. Rumination is rehashing events of the past in an unhealthy way. Worry is creating worst-case scenarios in a future that does not yet exist. If you are worrying or ruminating, you are not in the present moment.

2. Being present for someone else just as they are is a form of support.

3. Affirming someone's experience means that you acknowledge that person's experience without trying to change it, fix it or avoid it.

WORD WATERFALL

In this activity, the goal is to take what's in your head and get it out onto the page without any judgment at all. Just like you can't hold back a waterfall, you're not going to hold back anything that wants to come out.

Get your journal or a piece of paper and sketch an outline of a waterfall. Set a five-minute timer. You don't want to spend too much time on this; it's really just about getting it out as quickly as possible. Start the timer and in your waterfall, write down what is ready to come out. It could be simple words like "sad," "angry" or "happy." It could be names of people or pets. It could be colors, a song that has been in your head on repeat or a quick doodle of an object. It could be chores or homework assignments that you haven't done yet but are on your mind. You can also do scribbles. Let it flow!

Once the time is up, look at what you wrote down. Do you see any patterns or themes? Notice how you feel, and go back to the Keep Your Grief Moving activity at the end of

Chapter Five. Notice what is happening in your body and see if that connects to any feelings.

Listening to ourselves is something we have to learn how to do as we get older, and doing a brain dump like this is just one way of listening.

Chapter Nine

WHEN ADULTS GRIEVE

Do you know an adult who is grieving a deathloss or shadowloss? It can be hard to see someone you love hurting. It can also be scary to see a person who is usually in control and usually has all the answers need so much help. Adults grieve both deathlosses and shadowlosses just as kids do. There is no "on" or "off" switch for different types of grief just because of your age. Grief is grief.

You learned in Chapter One that grief is a response to loss. Behavioral, cognitive, emotional, physical, social and spiritual signs are parts of that grief response for both adults and kids. Adults can have signs in some or all of those categories just like you can.

Many grown-ups were taught that grief just means feeling really sad — or even that grief and sadness are the same thing. Sometimes they were taught that grief is a more intense kind of sadness. We know today that this isn't true. Sadness can be a part of grief, but sadness is not the same thing as grief. Though adults have had more practice with grief, they are still learning — and unlearning —ways for them to think and talk about it and move forward with it.

ADULTS DON'T ALL GRIEVE THE SAME

There is no such thing as "adult grief" or "kid grief." That is what can make it tricky sometimes. Every single person who is grieving has their own inside grief and outside grief. Your inside grief might need different things than your parent's does. And, every person (no matter their age) has their own set of unique grief signs. One adult might experience a lot of physical signs, while another might not really have any at all.

Still, you might feel uncomfortable, even sad, if your grief experience is different than an adult's experience in your life, especially if you are dealing with the same loss. But it doesn't mean you are any less close or that you cannot understand or comfort each other. It just means you have different ways of showing grief. That gives you a chance to learn from them — What comforts them? What is their grief energy? — and also teach them.

THE ONLY DiFFERENCE IS PRACTiCE

The one difference between an adult grieving and a kid grieving is that adults tend to have more experience with grief. Another way to say this is that most adults have had more practice with grief.

As I said in Chapter Four, if this is your first time grieving, it won't be your last. By the time you are 30, you will likely have lost 5–10 people. By the time you are 70, you might have lost 40 or more people.

By the time you are 70, you can think back to other times you grieved and can compare. You know you need to go for long walks every night, and you don't like talking about your feelings until you can do so without crying.

After 10 losses, you'll probably know what you need to feel supported as you move through the grief process. But at 10 years old, when it's your first grief experience — it's hard to know what to expect when you haven't done it before!

Do you remember the very first time you played a team sport? During your first game, everything was new. But after your fifth or tenth game you knew to wait for the coach before leaving the locker room. You knew stepping onto the court or field — no matter if it was a home or away game — always made your hands tremble, so you would have to give them a shake to get the strength back. You knew your heart rate would slow down by halftime. You knew what to expect and how to handle it.

When it comes to grief, the adults in your life likely have had more experience with it and so they have a better idea about what to expect. That's why it's helpful to tell adults you trust in your life how you are feeling and what your grief experience is like. They might be able to offer you help and comfort because they've been there before.

Everyone has a first game, a first love and a first big loss. It's normal for your first time with grief to feel extra intense or extra overwhelming. But even with practice, each experience has its challenges.

Adults who have experienced grief multiple times will still encounter challenging moments in their grieving process. That's partly because adults are still growing and changing as people, too. As a result, the way they grieve will change in some ways with each new loss. An interesting conversation to have with trusted adults is about the different ways they have grieved throughout their life. When they share their experience with you, it might make you feel less alone because they've been where you are before, and they got through it. You can also help them better understand what your experience is like. You might even find you have similar ways of experiencing grief and ways that are completely different. Grief is not something that can be fixed because nothing has broken. Grief is proof of love, and sharing our grief experience with each other can bring us closer.

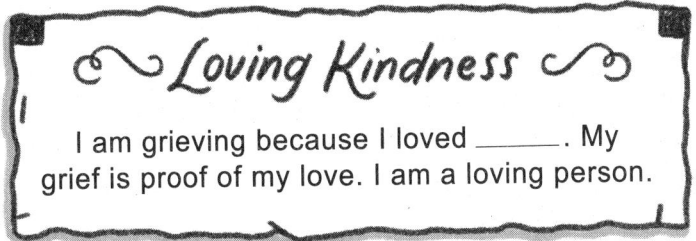

∾ *Loving Kindness* ∾

I am grieving because I loved _____. My grief is proof of my love. I am a loving person.

OTHER PEOPLE'S FEELINGS

When people are very good at being empathetic, they are also usually pretty good at being able to figure out when someone they care about isn't feeling good, even if that person doesn't directly say so. People who are empathetic sometimes have a special ability to say, "Hey, it seems like something is wrong; what's going on?" You might have heard people refer to this as a "sixth sense." That might be you.

Kids, especially, are attuned to the grown-ups they see regularly. This means kids can sense when the adults in their lives are feeling stressed or nervous, even if the adult denies it.

It's never your job to try to "fix" an adult's grief
(or anyone's grief, including your own). So what do
you do when you're worried about a grieving adult?

1. Tell that adult you're worried about them.

2. If nothing improves, talk to a trusted adult, like a close
   family member, neighbor, school counselor or teacher.

As a young person, it is not your responsibility to take
care of the adults in your life. It can help you and the
adult you care about to reach out to another trusted
adult and share your worries.

Adults take care of other adults, and adults also take
care of you.

It's really important to understand that you are not
responsible for the way that other people feel. As kids, it's
not your job to try to fix or change how other people are
feeling. What this means is that if someone you know is
feeling angry, it's okay for them to feel angry. You can ask
if they want to talk about why they are angry, but it's not
your responsibility to try and "solve" it and make their
anger go away.

You should ask someone how they are feeling if you
know or suspect they are going through something. You
can help them by offering to listen or simply by being near
them. You can ask them what they need. But you should not

"take on" their feelings. If they can't or won't do what they need — what their body and mind need — then it is not your responsibility to force them. Take care, don't take on.

When you see someone you care about sad and hurting, you feel sad and hurt for them. It can feel as though you are being more supportive by mirroring their emotions.

But just as we discussed in Chapter Two, someone else's loss is not yours. You can affirm their feelings, but you aren't being more empathetic, or a better support, if you bring yourself down or get yourself worked up as deeply as they do.

When it comes to grief within a family or household, sometimes you will be having a very good day while the grown-up is having a very bad day. You might feel full of energy, and you burst into the kitchen, excited to tell your dad that you feel ready to go to school for the first time in a week, only to see him crying at the stove.

That is normal.

So what should you do? Hide your good energy so your dad doesn't feel upset by it? Cheer up your dad so he can feel "better" like you do?

EXTRA HELP

CALL OR TEXT 988 IF YOU NEED SOMEONE TO TALK TO AND ARE IN THE UNITED STATES OR CANADA. THERE IS SOMEONE THERE FOR YOU 24/7.

It's not your job to put all your energy and focus into helping his bad day go away. If you are an empathetic person, it can be really hard to do this. But if someone you care about is having a bad day, it doesn't mean you also have to have a bad day.

What if you are having a bad day while other people are also having bad days? The most important thing to know is that if there is ever a day that you need help, or need to talk to someone, you should always tell them, even if they are having a bad day, too. It does not "add to their load." Remember, people often feel good when they can help others. The people who care about you want to help you, and it will always feel good for them to do so.

And if you are having a bad day while the adults in your life are having good days, you should always reach out when you need help or just want to talk. You won't make your bad day bleed into other people's good days.

Sometimes it might feel like you are abandoning your loved one by having a good day. That is just not true. Your feelings are your own, and other people's feelings are their own. It's always okay to share our feelings with those we trust, but it is not your job to fix or change the way that other people feel.

CONTINUE BEING YOU

We might want to hide our uncomfortable feelings from the adults in our life because we might think that's a way to help. It's important that you don't do this. Just because an adult in your life is grieving, you shouldn't make yourself smaller or hide parts of yourself. You are a whole person with your own experiences and feelings, just like the adults around you.

In times of grief, and all other times, you should always continue to be yourself. Changing yourself won't change the grief.

Carry this with you

1. Adults don't all grieve the same.
2. Adults usually have more practice with grief, but that doesn't mean that it's easier.
3. You are not responsible for other people's feelings. Take care, don't take on.
4. Adults are responsible for themselves and for your well-being.

MOOD TRACKER

If you want to take a scientific approach to your grief experience, you'll find the data you get from this mood tracker interesting. Get your journal or a piece of paper and draw three columns. At the top, label each column with the current month, the next month and the one after. Draw squares down each column — a month — for each day in that month. You'll need to assign a different color to each mood, like red for "angry" or blue for "sad." So, for example, if you felt really angry all day on December 1, you would color the box in red that corresponds to the December column and row 1. As every day goes by and you fill in each box with a color representing the most noticeable feeling you had that day, you will see patterns over time in your mood. Be sure to fill in those blank boxes with more feelings. You can also track your top two feelings each day by dividing each box in half (just draw a line down the center) or top four feelings by drawing a plus sign through each box. Science!

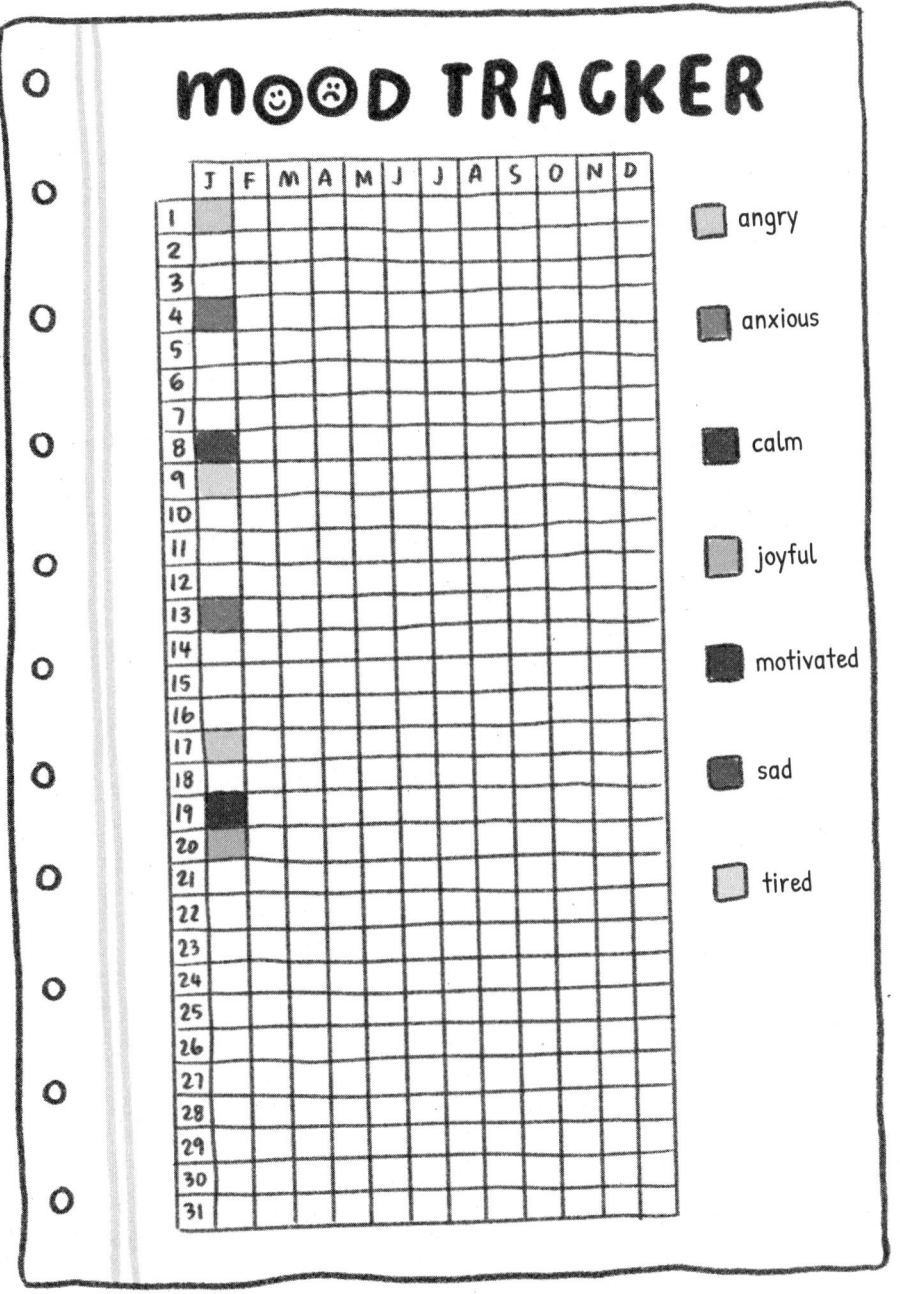

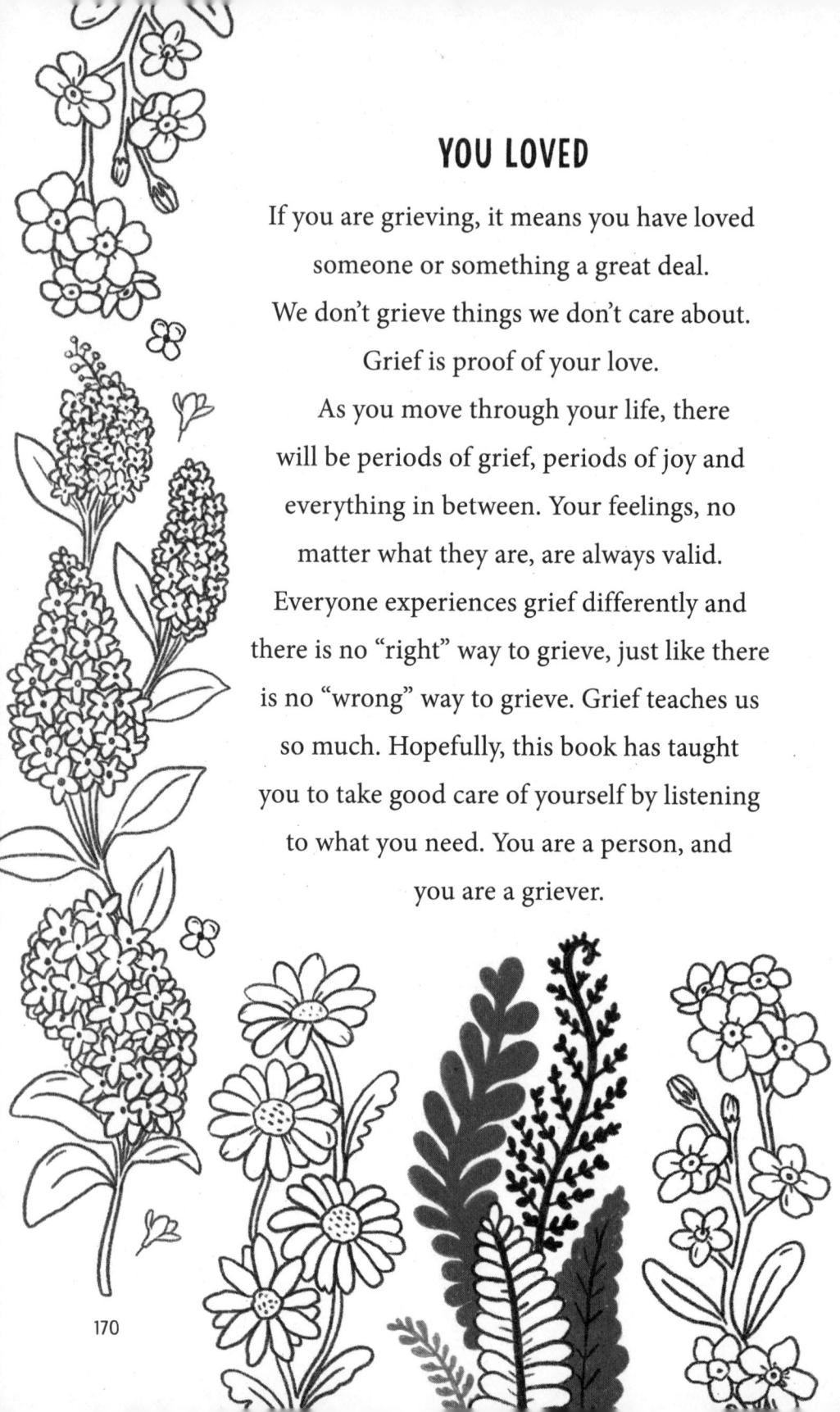

YOU LOVED

If you are grieving, it means you have loved someone or something a great deal.
We don't grieve things we don't care about.
Grief is proof of your love.
As you move through your life, there will be periods of grief, periods of joy and everything in between. Your feelings, no matter what they are, are always valid.
Everyone experiences grief differently and there is no "right" way to grieve, just like there is no "wrong" way to grieve. Grief teaches us so much. Hopefully, this book has taught you to take good care of yourself by listening to what you need. You are a person, and you are a griever.

GRIEF JOURNAL

Open your journal or a get a stack of papers. Below are a bunch of writing prompts. Write these down and answer them, or you can doodle your thoughts. The prompts are to help you think about some of the ideas discussed in this guide. They're to help you remember to connect to the world around you, to yourself and to your grief. You can also add photos, pressed flowers or stickers onto the pages. Journals can hold more than just written words!

WHAT HAS YOUR ↘ GRIEF ↙ EXPERIENCE BEEN LIKE?

What signs have you noticed from each of these categories: (see chapter 1)

COGNITIVE
BEHAVIORAL
EMOTIONAL
SOCIAL
SPIRITUAL
PHYSICAL

IS THIS YOUR FIRST GRIEF EXPERIENCE?

WHAT'S SOMETHING ABOUT THIS GRIEF EXPERIENCE THAT REALLY STICKS OUT TO YOU?

Use this page to make a list of **memories** of your loved one or of your Shadowloss. You can update the page any time you remember new things.

List 3 people who have really helped you during this time

How have they helped you?

How do they make you feel?

How do you appreciate them?

LIST 10 THINGS THAT ALWAYS SEEM TO CHEER YOU UP OR MAKE YOU FEEL BETTER NO MATTER WHAT

1.
2.
3.
4.
5.
6.
7.
8.
9.
10.

TODAY I'M MISSING

THIS IS A PAGE OF OPPORTUNITY

WHAT DO YOU HOPE FOR THE FUTURE?

GRiEF GLOSSARY

affirmation: a positive statement meant to uplift and support you

anticipatory grief: grief that appears before an expected deathloss or shadowloss

burial: the practice of burying a dead body

cognitive: relating to conscious intellectual activity

cremation: the practice of putting a dead body in fire until just the bones remain

deathloss: when a person or an animal we love dies

disposition: a choice for what you can do with a dead body. Common disposition methods are burial and cremation.

emotions and **feelings:** emotions are the body's response to a stimulus (to something that happens), and feelings occur when we become aware of those emotional reactions

empathy: the ability to understand and share the feelings of another person

eulogy: a piece of writing that is often read out loud that talks in an honest and heartfelt manner about a person who died

funeral: a ceremony or ritual in honor of a dead person

grief: whole-body response to loss, including physical, spiritual, social, cognitive, behavioral and emotional signs

grief energy: the differences you notice in the way you feel throughout the grief process

inside grief: all the ways we privately process and manage our grief

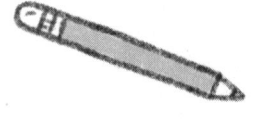

mourn: to feel deep sorrow over a deathloss or shadowloss. During the period of time when a person's grief is strongest, they are *in mourning*.

outside grief: all the ways we share and express our grief with others

presence: being able to be in the here and now

resilience: the ability to recover from a setback

ruminating: thinking of events that already happened, repeatedly and in a negative way

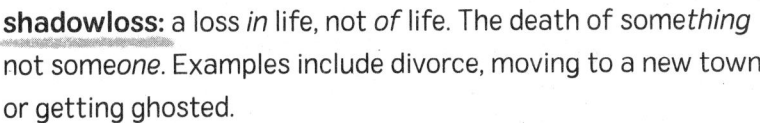

shadowloss: a loss *in* life, not *of* life. The death of some*thing* not some*one*. Examples include divorce, moving to a new town or getting ghosted.

symptoms or **signs:** physical or mental clues connected to a root cause. For example, a runny nose could be a physical symptom of allergies or a cold. The word symptom is used most often in a medical context to diagnose an illness. Grief is not an illness, so the word symptom isn't really accurate. Grief has signs; illnesses have symptoms.

toxic positivity: using overly positive language to avoid or ignore someone else's negative experience

worry: when the mind negatively focuses on things that could go wrong (but have not yet)

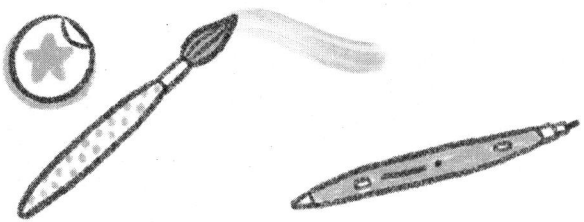

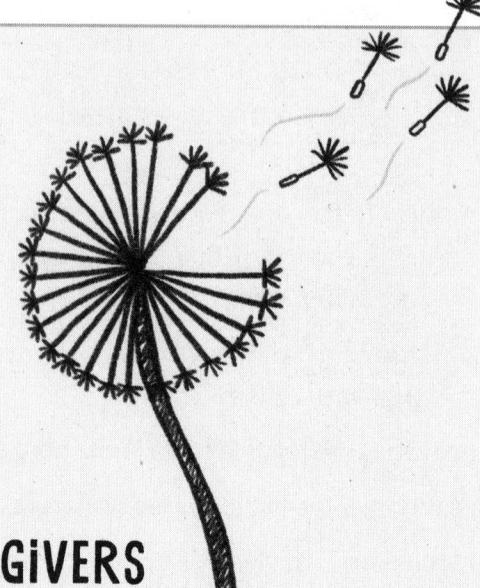

A NOTE FOR CAREGIVERS

In addition to the resources in this book,
there are a few basic things that can help you clearly and
safely communicate information to your child. When it
comes to the death of a person or animal, you'll want to
make sure you answer the following questions clearly and
directly. Avoid using indirect language like "passed away"
or "went to sleep"; those words might confuse young people
or make them imagine untrue scenarios. It's okay to say
someone died because that is the truth.

The three Cs, originally developed by Julie Stokes and later
expanded into the five Cs, offer a great template to follow
for important conversations about a loss. In studies done
over the years where clinicians interview bereaved children,
these young people most often experience two things:

feeling both responsible for the loss and cut off from communication about the loss. Therefore, when you talk to the young person in your life, start by answering these questions — even if they haven't been asked.

☐ Did I **cause** it?

☐ Can I **catch** it?

☐ Could I have **cured** it?

☐ Who is going to take **care** of me?

☐ How can I stay **connected** to the person?

A sixth **C** was developed by the Children and Youth Grief Network and is a great addition to the conversation:

☐ What is it **called**?

We learn how to talk about death from the adults we grew up around. So if you grew up hearing adults whisper the word "death" (or never even say it at all), then you might find you have a tendency to do that as well. Kids learn to fear death from adults; they don't learn that from other kids. You have an opportunity to change what your children might inherit here.

What makes these conversations tricky is not the questions they may have — more often than not it's how we handle the situation. Many parents and caregivers navigate their own issues related to death and dying when trying to companion a child through a loss. We're afraid of causing extra harm.

Just like you need to use clear language with children to help prevent imagination opportunities from running wild, you need to do that for yourself, too. In my experience over the years working with parents and caregivers, they also have excellent imaginations that are skilled at dreaming up all kinds of "what ifs" and worries with their own kids.

If it's important to you to model how to talk about difficult subjects, then that might require a little bravery and discomfort of your own. Even though you are an adult now with children of your own, you still have a little kid inside yourself who carries those early experiences with loss. Be gentle with yourself. You are doing the best you can with what you have and where you are. Ask for help. You can do this.

RESOURCES

This resource list includes websites, hotlines, books and videos.

For Kids and Caregivers
Websites and Articles

988 Suicide and Crisis Helpline (United States)

https://988lifeline.org

988 is available 24/7 in English and Spanish. The previous number (1-800-273-TALK) will continue to operate indefinitely.

Ball in a Jar Analogy

https://www.tandfonline.com/doi/abs/10.1080/02682629608657376

Dr. Lois Tonkin, in her 1996 article "Growing Around Grief: Another Way of Looking at Grief and Recovery," shared a helpful way of thinking about grief.

Ball in the Box Analogy

https://threadreaderapp.com/thread/946887540732149760.html

A great analogy for thinking about grief, shared by Lauren Herschel.

Camp Erin

https://elunanetwork.org/camps-programs/camp-erin

Camp Erin is the largest national bereavement program for youth grieving the death of a significant person in their lives. Camps are located across the United States with additional locations in Canada.

Dougy Center

https://www.dougy.org

The Dougy Center creates safe spaces and free resources for children and families who are grieving.

Fernside

https://www.fernside.org

Fernside is a center for grieving children in Cincinnati, Ohio; its website provides a lot of useful resources.

Kids Help Phone (Canada)

https://kidshelpphone.ca/our-e-mental-health-services/

Kids Help Phone's online mental health services are here 24/7 for people across Canada. The website provides details on the services offered and how users can get support with their mental health and well-being.

Refuge in Grief's Do This, Not That

https://refugeingrief.com/wp-content/uploads/2017/11/RiG _infogpraphic-DoThisNotThat-PrintReady.pdf

This handy, downloadable PDF by Megan Devine of Refuge in Grief covers what to do (and what not to do) when supporting a grieving person. Contact refugeingrief.com for permission to use or reprint.

Talk Suicide Canada

https://talksuicide.ca

Canadians can call or text 988 or call the 1-800-456-4566 hotline number. Service in English and French is available 24/7.

Talking About Mental Health (Explaining Depression and Anxiety)

https://www.youtube.com/watch?v=oz1S66_pYTw

This short video succinctly explains mental health.

The Compassionate Friends

https://compassionatefriends.org

This group supports families after a child dies. There are many local chapters in the United States and in over 30 other countries, as well as online support groups.

The Selah Carefarm/MISS Foundation
https://www.missfoundation.org/selah-carefarm/
This compassionate community offers therapeutic services and a
restorative environment in Sedona, Arizona, for the traumatically
bereaved.

Books
Griefabet: Everyday Letters to Wrap Around Your Heart
by Karen O. Johnson
Written with the individual griever in mind, *Griefabet* uses the
letters of the alphabet to offer comfort and encouragement to
anyone living with loss.

Grief Is a Mess by Jackie Schuld
This illustrated book is for grieving children and adults who need
a healthy dose of understanding, comfort and laughter. The book
explores how grief is different for everyone and can change
without warning.

When You Lose Someone You Love by Joanne Fink
This book feels like a genuine hug. It's just over 100 pages and
fully illustrated.

For Caregivers Only
Websites
American Academy of Child & Adolescent Psychiatry
https://www.aacap.org/AACAP/Families_and_Youth/Facts
_for_Families/FFF-Guide/Children-And-Grief-008.aspx
This link provides succinct information about how children can
respond to a death, including a list of things to keep an eye out
for when determining whether or not professional intervention
is needed.

Cole Imperi
https://www.coleimperi.com

Kids Grief
https://kidsgrief.ca
Caregivers and educators can find free online resources here.

**Shadowloss: Shedding Light on Our Hidden Grief
(a TEDx on Shadowloss)**
https://www.ted.com/talks/cole_imperi_shadowloss_shedding
_light_on_our_hidden_grief

The 6 Cs and the 3 Ws
https://www.childrenandyouthgriefnetwork.com
A succinct page explaining the 6 Cs and the 3 Ws, which can be
a helpful template for talking to kids about what's happening.

The Coalition to Support Grieving Students
https://grievingstudents.org/
This interdisciplinary group focusing on grieving students provides
downloadable grief support modules for school personnel.

The National Alliance for Children's Grief
https://nacg.org
If you are supporting a young griever, the NACG can connect you
to local support resources.

International Suicide Hotlines

This information was correct at the time of printing.
Please check online for the most up-to-date numbers in your area.

ALGERIA:
Emergency: 34342 and 43
Suicide Hotline: 0021 3983
2000 58

ARGENTINA:
Emergency: 911
Suicide Hotline: 135

ARMENIA:
Emergency: 911 and 112
Suicide Hotline: (2) 538194

AUSTRALIA:
Emergency: 000
Suicide Hotline: 13 11 14

AUSTRIA:
Emergency: 112
Telefonseelsorge 24/7: 142
Rat auf Draht
24/7: 147 (Youth)

BAHAMAS:
Emergency: 911
Suicide Hotline: (2) 322-2763

BAHRAIN:
Emergency: 999

BANGLADESH:
Emergency: 999

BARBADOS:
Emergency: 911
Suicide Hotline: Samaritan
Barbados (246) 4299999

BELGIUM:
Emergency: 112
Suicide Hotline: Stichting
Zelfmoordlijn 1813

BOLIVIA:
Emergency: 911
Suicide Hotline: 3911270

BOSNIA & HERZEGOVINA:
Suicide Hotline: 080 05 03 05

BOTSWANA:
Emergency: 911
Suicide Hotline: +2673911270

BRAZIL:
Emergency: 188

BULGARIA:
Emergency: 112
Suicide Hotline: 0035 9249 17 223

CANADA:
Emergency: 911
Suicide Hotline: 988

CHINA:
Emergency: 110
Suicide Hotline: 800-810-1117

COLOMBIA:
24/7 Helpline in Barranquilla:
1(00 57 5) 372 27 27
24/7 Hotline Bogota: (57-1) 323 24 25

CROATIA:
Emergency: 112

CYPRUS:
Emergency: 112
Suicide Hotline: 8000 7773

CZECH REPUBLIC:
Emergency: 112

DENMARK:
Emergency: 112
Suicide Hotline: 4570201201

EGYPT:
Emergency: 122
Suicide Hotline: 762 1602

ESTONIA:
Emergency: 112
Suicide Hotline: 3726558088;
in Russian 3726555688

ETHIOPIA:
Emergency: 911

FINLAND:
Emergency: 112
Suicide Hotline: 09 2525 0111

FRANCE:
Emergency: 112
Suicide Hotline: 0145394000

GERMANY:
Emergency: 112
Suicide Hotline: 08001810771

GHANA:
Emergency: 999
Suicide Hotline: 2332 444 71279

GREECE:
Emergency: 112
Suicide Hotline: 1018

GUYANA:
Emergency: 999
Suicide Hotline: 223-0001

HONG KONG:
Emergency: 999
Suicide Hotline: 852 2382 0000

HUNGARY:
Emergency: 112
Suicide Hotline: 116123

INDIA:
Emergency: 112
Suicide Hotline: 8888817666

INDONESIA:
Emergency: 112
Suicide Hotline: 1-800-273-8255

IRAN:
Emergency: 110
Suicide Hotline: 1480

IRELAND:
Emergency: 112 and 999
Suicide Hotline: 116 123

ISRAEL:
Emergency: 100
Suicide Hotline: 1201

ITALY:
Emergency: 112
Suicide Hotline: 800860022

JAMAICA:
Emergency: 911
Suicide Hotline: 888-639-5433

JAPAN:
Emergency: 110
Suicide Hotline: 810352869090

JORDAN:
Emergency: 911
Suicide Hotline: 110

KENYA:
Emergency: 999
Suicide Hotline: 722178177

KUWAIT:
Emergency: 112
Suicide Hotline: 94069304

LATVIA:
Emergency: 113
Suicide Hotline: 371 67222922

LEBANON:
Suicide Hotline: 1564

LIBERIA:
Emergency: 911
Suicide Hotline: 6534308

LUXEMBOURG:
Emergency: 112
Suicide Hotline: 352 45 45 45

MALAYSIA:
Emergency: 999
Suicide Hotline: (06) 2842500

MALTA:
Suicide Hotline: 179

MAURITIUS:
Emergency: 112
Suicide Hotline: +230 800 93 93

MEXICO:
Emergency: 911
Suicide Hotline: 5255102550

NETHERLANDS:
Emergency: 112
Suicide Hotline: 0800-0113

NEW ZEALAND:
Emergency: 111
Suicide Hotline: 1737

NIGERIA:
Suicide Hotline: 234 8092106493

NORWAY:
Emergency: 112
Suicide Hotline: +4781533300

PAKISTAN:
Emergency: 115

PHILIPPINES:
Emergency: 911
Suicide Hotline: 028969191

POLAND:
Emergency: 112
Suicide Hotline: 5270000

PORTUGAL:
Emergency: 112
Suicide Hotline: 21 854 07 40
and 8 96 898 21 50

QATAR:
Emergency: 999

ROMANIA:
Emergency: 112
Suicide Hotline: 0800 801200

RUSSIA:
Emergency: 112
Suicide Hotline: 0078202577577

**SAINT VINCENT AND
THE GRENADINES:**
Suicide Hotline: 9784 456 1044

SAUDI ARABIA:
Emergency: 112

SERBIA:
Suicide Hotline: (+381) 21-6623-393

SINGAPORE:
Emergency: 999
Suicide Hotline: 1 800 2214444

SOUTH AFRICA:
Emergency: 10111
Suicide Hotline: 0514445691

SOUTH KOREA:
Emergency: 112
Suicide Hotline: (02) 7158600

SPAIN:
Emergency: 112
Suicide Hotline: 914590050

SRI LANKA:
Suicide Hotline: 011 057 2222662

SUDAN:
Suicide Hotline: (249) 11-555-253

SWEDEN:
Emergency: 112
Suicide Hotline: 46317112400

SWITZERLAND:
Emergency: 112
Suicide Hotline: 143

TANZANIA:
Emergency: 112

THAILAND:
Suicide Hotline: (02) 713-6793

TONGA:
Suicide Hotline: 23000

TRINIDAD AND TOBAGO:
Suicide Hotline: (868) 645 2800

TUNISIA:
Emergency: 197

TURKEY:
Emergency: 112

UGANDA:
Emergency: 112
Suicide Hotline: 0800 21 21 21

UNITED ARAB EMIRATES:
Suicide Hotline: 800 46342

UNITED KINGDOM:
Emergency: 112
Suicide Hotline: 0800 689 5652

UNITED STATES:
Emergency: 911
Suicide Hotline: 988

ZAMBIA:
Emergency: 999
Suicide Hotline: +260960264040

ZIMBABWE:
Emergency: 999
Suicide Hotline: 080 12 333 333

References

Books

- Barrett, Lisa Feldman. *How Emotions Are Made: The Secret Life of the Brain*. New York: Houghton Mifflin Harcourt, 2017.

- Goldblatt Hyatt, Erica. *Grieving for the Sibling You Lost: A Teen's Guide to Coping with Grief and Finding Meaning After Loss*. Oakland, CA: Instant Help Books, 2015.

- Kübler-Ross, Elisabeth. *On Children and Death: How Children and Their Parents Can and Do Cope with Death*. New York: Scribner, 1997.

- McNiel, Andy, and Pamela Gabbay. *Understanding and Supporting Bereaved Children: A Practical Guide for Professionals*. New York: Springer, 2017.

- Servaty-Seib, Heather L., and Helen S. Chapple, eds. *The Handbook of Thanatology: The Essential Body of Knowledge for the Study of Death, Dying, and Bereavement*, Third Edition. Association for Death Education and Counseling, 2021.

- Worden, James William. *Children and Grief: When a Parent Dies*. New York: Guilford Press, 1996.

Journals

- Albuquerque, Sara, and Ana R. Santos. "'In the Same Storm, but Not on the Same Boat': Children Grief During the COVID-19 Pandemic." *Frontiers in Psychiatry* 12 (January 26, 2021).

- Barrett, Lisa Feldman. "Emotions Are Real." *Emotion* 12, no. 3 (2012): 413–29.

- Basky, Greg. "Canada Will Have Three-Digit Suicide Prevention Hotline by 2023." *Canadian Medical Association Journal* 193, no. 3 (January 18, 2021): E106–7.

- Bassett, Debra J. "Who Wants to Live Forever? Living, Dying and Grieving in Our Digital Society." *Social Sciences* 4, no. 4 (December 2015): 1127–39.

- Dyregrov, Atle, Alison Salloum, Pål Kristensen, and Kari Dyregrov. "Grief and Traumatic Grief in Children in the Context of Mass Trauma." *Current Psychiatry Reports* 17, no. 6 (May 6, 2015): 48.

- Fitzgerald, Dominic A., Kenneth Nunn, and David Isaacs. "What We Have Learnt about Trauma, Loss and Grief for Children in Response to COVID-19." *Paediatric Respiratory Reviews* 39 (September 1, 2021): 16–21.

- Flahault, Cécile, S. Dolbeault, C. Sankey, and L. Fasse. "Understanding Grief in Children Who Have Lost a Parent with Cancer: How Do They Give Meaning to This Experience? Results of an Interpretative Phenomenological Analysis." *Death Studies* 42, no. 8 (September 14, 2018): 483–90.

- Freedman, Gili, Darcey N. Powell, Benjamin Le, and Kipling D. Williams. "Ghosting and Destiny: Implicit Theories of Relationships Predict Beliefs about Ghosting." *Journal of Social and Personal Relationships* 36, no. 3 (2019): 905–924.

- Her-Xiong, Youhung and Tracy Schroepfer. "Walking in Two Worlds: Hmong End-of-Life Beliefs & Rituals." *Journal of Social Work in End-of-Life & Palliative Care* 14, no. 4 (2018): 291–314.

- Librach, S. L. "Supporting Children's Grief within an Adult and Pediatric Palliative Care Program." *Journal of Supportive Oncology* 9, no. 4 (2011): 136–140

- Miller, Mark D. "Complicated Grief in Late Life." *Dialogues in Clinical Neuroscience* 14, no. 2 (June 30, 2012): 195–202.

- Nummenmaa, Lauri, Enrico Glerean, Riitta Hari, and Jari K. Hietanen. "Bodily Maps of Emotions." *Proceedings of the National Academy of Sciences of the United States of America* 111, no. 2 (January 14, 2014): 646–51.

- Peters, Joey. "Protecting the Living While Serving the Dead, Hmong Funerals Adapt to COVID-19 Times." *Sahan Journal*, December 3, 2020.

- Simonsen, Lone, and Cecile Viboud. "A Comprehensive Look at the COVID-19 Pandemic Death Toll." *eLife* 10 (August 12, 2021): e71974.

- Stokes, J., "Anticipatory Grief in Families Affected by HIV/AIDS," *Progress in Palliative Care* 2 (1994): 43–48.

- Verdery, Ashton M., Emily Smith-Greenaway, Rachel Margolis, and Jonathan Daw. "Tracking the Reach of COVID-19 Kin Loss with a Bereavement Multiplier Applied to the United States." *Proceedings of the National Academy of Sciences* 117, no. 30 (July 28, 2020): 17695–701.

- Wiegand, Debra, and In Seo La. "Bereavement Interventions for Grieving Family Members: A Systematic Review (S874)." *Journal of Pain and Symptom Management* 57, no. 2 (February 1, 2019): 521–22.

Websites and Articles

- AACAP. "Grief and Children." Accessed July 25, 2022. https://www.aacap.org/AACAP/Families_and_Youth/Facts_for_Families/FFF-Guide/Children-And-Grief-008.aspx.

- Anna Freud National Centre for Children and Families. "Talking Mental Health (subtitled), 2017." https://www.youtube.com/watch?v=oz1S66_pYTw.

- Beck, Julie. "Hard Feelings: Science's Struggle to Define Emotions," *The Atlantic*, February 24, 2015. https://www.theatlantic.com/health/archive/2015/02/hard-feelings-sciences-struggle-to-define-emotions/385711/

- Brain Tumour Foundation of Canada. "Understanding the Five C's of Children's Grief," March 2, 2021. https://www.braintumour.ca/blog/support/understanding-the-five-cs-of-childrens-grief/.

- Center for Grieving Children. "Physical Manifestations of Grief," July 16, 2019. https://www.cgcmaine.org/2019/07/16/physical-manifestations-of-grief/.

- "Childhood Bereavement Estimation Model." Judi's House (blog). Accessed July 25, 2022. https://judishouse.org/research-tools/cbem/.

- Children and Youth Grief Network. "Education Support Resources." Accessed July 25, 2022. https://www.childrenandyouthgriefnetwork.com/.

- Dougy Center. "Grief Feels Like." Accessed July 25, 2022. https://www.dougy.org/videos/grief-feels-like.

- EKR Foundation. "Dr. Elisabeth Kübler-Ross and the Five Stages of Grief®." Accessed July 25, 2022. https://www.ekrfoundation.org/5-stages-of-grief/5-stages-grief/.

- Fernside Center for Grieving Children. "Resource Library." Accessed July 25, 2022. https://www.fernside.org/grief-resources/booklists-referrals.

- Funeralwise. "Atheist Funeral Service Rituals." Accessed July 25, 2022. https://www.funeralwise.com/funeral-customs/atheist/.

- Green, Emma. "Burying Your Dead Without Religion." *The Atlantic*, August 19, 2014. https://www.theatlantic.com/national/archive/2014/08/burying-your-dead-without-religion/378711/

- "Hmong Traditional Funerals." Accessed July 25, 2022. https://religionsmn.carleton.edu/exhibits/show/hmong-religiosity/hmong-rituals-birth-marriage-d/hmong-traditional-funerals.

- Kavod v'Nichum. "Honoring Death in Life." Accessed July 25, 2022. https://kavodvnichum.org/.

- KidsHealth New Zealand. "Bereavement Reactions of Children & Young People by Age Group." September 13, 2011. https://www.kidshealth.org.nz/bereavement-reactions-children-young-people-age-group.

- Kübler-Ross, Elisabeth. *The Dougy Letter*. Elisabeth Kübler-Ross Foundation, 1981. Additional Information: https://www.dougy.org/about/our-story/our-inspiration

- National Alliance for Children's Grief. "Grief Support Resource Library." Accessed June 2, 2022. https://nacg.org/resource-library/.

- *Psychology Today.* "What Do We Know About Ghosting?" Accessed October 28, 2019. https://www.psychologytoday.com/blog/close-encounters/201803/what-do-we-know-about-ghosting.

- Scientific American. "Feeling Our Emotions." Accessed July 25, 2022. https://www.scientificamerican.com/article/feeling-our-emotions/.

- Sesame Workshop. "Grief." Accessed June 16, 2019. https://sesameworkshop.org/topics/grief/.

- *Washington Post.* "Perspective | I Had No Idea How to Talk to My Children About a Loved One's Death. I'm Not Alone." Accessed July 25, 2022. https://www.washingtonpost.com/health/talking-about-death-to-kids/2021/08/13/2c2fbcf2-efd1-11eb-a452-4da5fe48582d_story.html.

- *Washington Post.* "The Big Number: 1.5 Million Children Worldwide Have Lost a Parent or Primary Caregiver Due to Covid-19." Accessed July 25, 2022. https://www.washingtonpost.com/health/covid-orphans/2021/07/23/706ed26e-eafd-11eb-97a0-a09d10181e36_story.html.

INDEX

affirmation, 154–155
anger, 56, 59, 82–83
animals
  experiencing grief, 115–116
  grief for, 32, 48–50, 92
  sharing grief with, 116–117
anticipatory grief, 33
appetite/eating, 24, 29

Bryant, Kobe, 55
Buddhist rituals, 139
burial, 41, 46

chaplains, 4
communication. *see* talking
COVID-19 pandemic, 67–68
cremation, 41–42
crying, 31, 88
the Cs, 176–177

death
  discomfort around, 15–17, 60
  inevitability of, 59–60
deathloss
  defined, 39–42, 51–52
  during COVID-19 pandemic, 68
  of famous people, 54–55
  questions around, 58–60
  relationship after, 57
  rituals for, 41–50, 138–143
  talking about, 176–178
disposition, 41
divorce, 67, 69
drinking water, 28

eating/appetite, 24, 29
emotions
  anger, 56, 59, 82–83
  feelings vs., 102–103
  of grief, 31
  sadness, 88, 108
  see also feelings

empathy, 129–130, 131–132, 163–167
eulogies, 46

feelings
  in animals, 115
  avoiding, 81–86, 101, 109–111, 153–154
  changeability of, 99–100, 106
  emotions vs., 102–103
  flowchart of, 118–119
  hiding, 165–167
  overwhelm, 148–149
  paying attention to, 79, 82–83, 102–103
  responsibility for, 164–166
  right to exist of, 104–106
  sharing, 106–107, 112–115, 116–117
  weather as metaphor, 106–108
  see also emotions; grief energy
funerals, 41–50

ghosting, 67
gratitude, 36–37, 60–61
grief
  in adults, 159–167
  for animals, 32, 48–50, 92
  animals experiencing, 115–116
  anticipatory grief, 33
  defined, 18–19
  experience with, 41, 78, 161–162
  feelings of, 31, 99–119
  feelings vs., 18–19, 104, 160
  finding meaning in, 122–133
  helping others through, 114–115, 147–155,
    164, 176–178
  individuality of, 18–19, 34, 53–54, 105, 160–161
  inevitability of, 18, 41, 77
  outside and inside grief, 137–143
  as process, 18, 121–122
  for public figures, 54–55
  responses of others to, 4, 12, 30
  signs of, 20–31, 122–123
  taking breaks from, 85, 109–110, 112, 114
  talking about, 15–17, 30–31, 149–155

types of, 4
universality of, 15, 77
see also deathloss; shadowloss
grief, coping with
funerals as medicine, 42–44, 49–50
getting help with, 13, 25, 163, 166
healing from, 121–135
keeping grief moving, 84–97
loving life, 60–61
paying attention to feelings, 79–83
physical aspects, 24, 27–28
resources, 179–186
sharing feelings, 106–107, 112–115, 116–117
spiritual aspects, 25–26
taking up space, 53–54
see also grief exercises
grief energy, 77–97
described, 77, 79–81
keeping grief moving, 84–97
paying attention to, 81–83
unfamiliarity of, 78
grief exercises
beaming love into self (visualization),
134–135
flowchart of feelings, 118–119
grief journal, 172–173
inside and outside grief, 141–142
lighting a candle, 62–63
mood tracker, 168–169
rainbow of gratitude, 36–37
sacred spots, 74–75
word waterfall, 156–157
your community of care, 144–145
grief medicine, 42–44, 49–50
grief rituals
for deathloss, 41–50, 138–143
effect of COVID-19 pandemic on, 68
for shadowloss, 70, 74–75
see also grief exercises

Hindu rituals, 139
Hmong rituals, 45–46

inside grief, 137, 141

Kaddish (Jewish prayer), 138–139

listening, 149–150
see also talking

mourning, 43

outside grief, 137–143
overwhelm, 148–149

pets. *see* animals
presence
defined, 130, 147–149
paying attention to feelings, 82–83
supporting others with, 149–150

resilience, 124, 129, 130–131
ruminating, 147

sadness, 88, 108
Sagan, Carl, 42
shadowloss
defined, 4, 65–66
examples of, 66–69, 71
grieving, 70–73
ritual for, 74–75
sleep, 27–28
spirituality, 25–26, 122–133
Stokes, Julie, 176
stress, 23, 29
sympathy, 129–130

talking
about death, 176–178
about grief, 15–17, 30–31, 149–155
sharing feelings, 106–107, 112–115, 116–117
thanatologists, 4
toxic positivity, 153–154
traditions. *see* grief rituals

"why" questions, 58
worrying, 147–148

ACKNOWLEDGMENTS

Writing this book has been a gift and a complex experience in and of itself. The process of writing a book will highlight all of your weaknesses and shortcomings, and it will also highlight the people in your life who love and care about you. Grief can be a disorienting, confusing and unfamiliar experience with no end in sight — I have found that with writing a book, too! I had challenging days during this process when I doubted myself sometimes, and I worried more than was probably necessary about the risk of potentially letting my readers down. Just like with grief, you get through it. And just like with grief, the process will probably be a little messy and uncomfortable, despite all the planning in the world.

I'd like to acknowledge the people, animals and plants that helped shape me into the person I am today, that invested their time and love into me and that walked the path with me as I became a thanatologist.

Victor Imperi: In 2024, we celebrate 17 years of marriage and 21 years together. I am so happy that I get to be your wife. We have grown up together and grown together. You know me better than I know myself and are generous with your love every single day. You have cared for my heart during this process and witnessed me at my worst and my best. You've always believed in me and have walked beside me as I built and navigated my career. Thank you for your loving support, the sacrifices you've made along the way and your patience. You are my best friend and the love of my life.

Patricia Ocampo: Growing up, I used to play *The Legend of Zelda* on Super Nintendo. There are parts in the game where Link — the main character — can visit Fairy Fountains and get all of his hearts restored, restoring his body, mind and soul. This has been my experience with you, Patricia! You are an exceptionally talented editor, and not just with words on the page but feelings in the heart. Thank you for your skill, professionalism, heart and humor.

Kids Can Press: Thank you for publishing this book, for believing in kids' ability to understand complex aspects of life and for your embrace of challenging and meaningful subjects.

Stacey Kondla of The Rights Factory: Thank you for your thoughtful care and commitment to this book and for finding it a home. Your excitement about books and the future of publishing is inspiring.

Heather Bokon and Jaclyn Lynch: Your administrative support helped hide my professional weaknesses from the world. Thank you for everything you have done to keep my i's dotted and my t's crossed. I am grateful to you both.

Erin Malone of WME: It takes a special person to see the potential that you do in a thanatologist from Kentucky! Thank you for your excitement about my work and for your earnest and keen approach to literary endeavors. I am grateful to have your voice in my world.

The students of the School of American Thanatology: You've accompanied me in this book-writing process in more ways than you'll know! Thank you for sharing your experiences with me, for passing along articles and studies, and for making efforts to remain connected to our school's community during a time when connection has seemed nearly impossible. I am grateful to all of you.

Those who have died: Many people I love have died. Their presence in my life continues to be felt, and their influence on me remains. Thank you to Aunt Susan, Grandma, Grandpa, Lucerne, Grandma Iris, Cindy Imperi, Leo Imperi, Carol Rose, Jessica Safran, Bob Luebbers, my sister Christina, Duncan, Drennen, Elkie, Preston, Brooklyn, Nora, Dana, Quillie, Sophie, Shelly, Moose Simpson, Donny Gilreath,

Shauna Bracher, Bubba Hoctor (JKL), Kathryn Lee Brickman, my Death Companioning clients, my hospice clients and Ruby and Hairy for all that you have taught me about death, dying, grief and loss. Your memories are blessings.

Mom and Dad: Thank you for being excited about what I do and for your words of encouragement. Thank you for the wonderful childhood my adulthood is rooted in. I don't think I personally could sustain a career in and around such a challenging subject if I hadn't had that gift. I could not do this without all that you gave me growing up.

Kristen Burgoyne, Emily Paver and Alie Ward: You listened to me as I figured out navigating the process of writing a book and offered me encouragement along the way.

Daisy: You've made life better, and I'm so lucky I get to be your person.

The daisy, the fern, the violet and the iris: Thank you to these thanabotanical plants for accompanying me these last few years as I navigated various shadowlosses and deathlosses.

The Lloyd Library, The Mercantile Library and Historic Linden Grove Cemetery and Arboretum: Thank you for being physical spaces housing supportive people who fostered me in various ways. Parts of this book were written in each of these locations.

The National Society of Newspaper Columnists:
Thank you for facilitating and nurturing a unique flavor of camaraderie that has completely enriched my life and made writing a lot less lonely.

Dr. James Ellis and the St. Elizabeth Community Grief Center: Thank you for facilitating opportunities to serve grieving folks of all ages, and for your mentorship.

Those experiencing incarceration at the Hamilton County Justice Center in Cincinnati, Ohio: Thank you for the opportunity to be a tiny part of your lives. In my role there as a chaplain, you shared openly with me about your shadowlosses and deathlosses. I believe in you.

The Elisabeth Kübler-Ross Foundation: Thank you for your support of and belief in my work and for your efforts to preserve the legacy of my favorite thanatologist — Elisabeth Kübler-Ross.

Judaism is central to my identity, and it nurtures some of the best parts of my life: connection, ritual and meaning. I would like to acknowledge a few of the spiritual places that have housed me throughout my life and were central to my thanatological formation: **The New York Zen Center for Contemplative Care, the New York Open Center, the Himalayan Institute, Congregation B'nai Tikvah,**

St. Saviour School and the Department of Judaic Studies at the University of Cincinnati as well as Hebrew Union College, Cincinnati.

My writing teachers: Thank you to Jim Tinsley and Liz Wrocklage-Gonda, two of my high-school English teachers. Mr. Tinsley — you were the first teacher to take my writing seriously, which allowed me to take my writing seriously. Ms. Wrocklage-Gonda — you showed me how writing could be woven into other parts of your life's journey and that it didn't have to be an either/or option — it could be a both/and choice. Thank you to Cheralyn Jardine, my high-school journalism teacher and school newspaper adviser. You taught me that writing could be part of a career, and that I was good enough to write. I learned about being edited and how to tell a story to others. You took extra time with me during some very difficult teenage years and provided a respite then that I still benefit from today. Thank you to Jenny Wohlfarth, my magazine journalism professor at the University of Cincinnati. You showed me how to strengthen my writing and how to get my words in front of different audiences. Finally, thank you to WMUL-FM 88.1 in Huntington, West Virginia, where I learned to put my own voice behind my words.

Peer review team: Thank you to Dr. Simcha Raphael, Wilka Roig, Dailyn Rodriguez, Alie Ward, Kristen Burgoyne, Ken Ross, Dr. Katie Eastman, and Mandy Benoualid for reviewing this work before it was finished. Your feedback made this book a safer place for grievers to inhabit.

Finally, thank you to the people who spend some of their lives with me online. The time you take to message me through my website or social media is meaningful to me. Thank you for connecting.

May we all keep our grief moving!